The Agile Equilibrium

The Agile Equilibrium

Balancing Organizational Freedom and Structure

Tommaso Balbo di Vinadio

BEP

BUSINESS EXPERT PRESS

Leader in applied, concise business books

The Agile Equilibrium: Balancing Organizational Freedom and Structure

Cover design by Louise Longeau

Interior design by Exeter Premedia Services Private Ltd., Chennai, India

First published in 2025 by
Business Expert Press, LLC
222 East 46th Street, New York, NY 10017
www.businessexpertpress.com

ISBN-13: 978-1-63742-754-5 (paperback)
ISBN-13: 978-1-63742-755-2 (e-book)

Business Expert Press Human Resource Management and Organizational Behavior Collection

First edition: 2025

10 9 8 7 6 5 4 3 2 1

Description

Have you ever felt frustrated by bureaucratic red tape or found management theories too abstract to apply? *The Agile Equilibrium: Balancing Organizational Freedom and Structure* **is your guide to navigating these challenges with practical, actionable insights.**

This book demystifies the complexities of management, offering a framework that harmonizes freedom and structure—two critical elements for organizations and teams facing the rapid pace of technological change.

Drawing on the latest research and the author's experience across the public, private, and academic sectors, this book provides real-world examples and best practices at the organizational, team, and individual levels. Whether you're a manager looking to boost team dynamics, an entrepreneur striving for organizational agility, or a student eager to master key management principles, **this book is an essential resource for enhancing both workplace satisfaction and productivity.**

Contents

Testimonials

"Tommaso Balbo di Vinadio has done something remarkable. He has combined his global management experience across different sectors with insights from practices at the world's best organizations. His "agile equilibrium" helps guide us to succeed as leaders in a more and more complex world. It shows us how high-performing teams and organizations can strike the right balance between freedom and structure."—**Bidjan Nashat, Co-Founder PotentialU, Former CEO at Atlas and Senior Executive at Save the Children**

"The Agile Equilibrium *is a must-read for managers and leaders committed to building agile, high-performing organizations in both the private and public sectors. Tommaso Balbo di Vinadio masterfully bridges the gap between organizational structure and autonomy—one of the most pressing challenges in modern management. The book presents a practical framework for leaders who want to foster a culture of innovation and drive impactful change. Highly recommended!"*—**Stefano Mastrogiacomo, author of *High-Impact Tools for Teams***

"Agile Equilibrium *is a must-read for managers seeking to foster innovation and productivity. It offers a wealth of theoretical knowledge combined with practical guidance and actionable insights illustrated by real-world case studies. By exploring the delicate balance between freedom and structure, this book will empower organizations to achieve exceptional results by reaching their full potential."*—**Mareta Alieva, Media Partnerships at Meta**

Preface

What Is This Book About?

This book concisely introduces a management framework that strikes a balance between freedom and structure—an agile equilibrium—which is crucial for organizations (and teams and individuals) who need to navigate today's fast-paced technological landscape, building on the existing literature and building on the author's work experience working for public service, private sector, and academia. It also addresses the challenges that organizations face when they are overly structured or excessively free.

By integrating autonomy with clear goals and accountability, the book showcases ways to enhance innovation and performance at both organizational and team levels, using practical examples. It also shows how this equilibrium between autonomy and structure can make people feel genuinely fulfilled and happy. Therefore, the book aims to identify some good practices for organizations and teams to adopt.

The book will primarily focus on exploring key concepts and strategies rather than providing a complete set of tools and checklists. For those seeking more detailed guidance, including specific solutions and checklists, those will be soon available on the author's website (www.tommasobalbo.com/) and in a forthcoming book, which will delve deeper into specific strategies and methods for enhancing organizational agility and team effectiveness.

Elevator pitch: Have you ever felt frustrated by bureaucracy or found management concepts too abstract? This book simplifies the complex world of management and addresses common workplace frustrations such as unclear goals and stifling bureaucracy. By presenting a clear, actionable framework, it demonstrates how some organizations have successfully developed some practices that balanced clarity over objectives with employee autonomy, and how, even in traditional organizations, fostering thriving teams and high-performing environments was possible. Dive into a narrative filled with tangible examples, making it an ideal read for anyone eager to see theory put into practice and improve both satisfaction and productivity at work.

Key messages of the book include the following:

- The large majority of organizations, whether private or public, need to become more agile and flexible, in order to stay competitive and/or to address increasingly complex challenges in today's fast-paced, technology-driven landscape.
- Great companies achieve success by balancing structure (clear missions, roles, and objectives) with freedom (autonomy and collaboration), cultivating a culture where innovation and accountability can harmoniously coexist.
- Organizations need to be fundamentally people-centric—they create environments that recognize and embrace the full humanity of their employees.
- When employees are given enough autonomy and are empowered while having some overall guidance and structure, they are more motivated and productive.
- Many high-performing teams have devised specific practices to strike this balance, and use them to take decisions, and make meetings more dynamic and productive.
- Communication and trust are foundational elements in achieving this equilibrium between freedom and structure.
- It's crucial to tailor these principles to fit the unique needs of each organization or team, recognizing the interplay between exploration and exploitation—not all organizations or teams need to apply the same principles in the same way.

- Traditional organizations can also develop high-performing teams by applying these insights.
- Leadership, at all levels, plays a critical role in fostering a culture that balances structure with freedom; it will thus play a major role in the application of these principles.

What This Book Is Not About

The book references well-researched works and the author's experience, but it does not aim to offer a groundbreaking theoretical contribution based on extensive research. Other books have researched several of the dimensions this book focuses on better, and more rigorously.

While it highlights practices from great organizations, the book does not claim to present a comprehensive view of these companies nor does it claim to endorse or advocate for those companies. Instead, it shares effective strategies for performance enhancement. Indeed, the "great companies" mentioned in this book are used as "archetypes," to show how they have managed to find a good balance between structure and freedom.

Who Is This Book For?

Primary readers will include:

(a) Middle to senior managers in large organizations, who stand to gain significantly from this book, as it provides strategies that will help to balance structure with the autonomy necessary for innovation and responding to rapid changes, thus enhancing their ability to lead effective teams.

(b) Younger executives in start-ups, who can benefit from understanding how to establish clear objectives and accountability while maintaining the flexibility and creativity critical for start-up growth and

(c) Master's students in management and related fields who want to understand complex concepts in a simplified manner.

The book is designed to fill the gap in management literature, providing clear, accessible insights into organizational and team dynamics without the dense jargon typical of traditional texts or management books.

How to Read This Book

The book adopts a unique format, presenting its insights in an informal style that makes readers feel like they are part of the discussion. This approach aims to make the content engaging and accessible, using an informal tone as if you are having a chat with the author. The conversational structure mirrors the author's thought process, reflecting a reflective and inquisitive style. This method helps explore management concepts in depth, encouraging readers to engage with the material dynamically and open-mindedly.

To enhance engagement and provide clarity, each chapter begins with a list of headers, which allow to quickly grasp the main ideas and find their precise locations within the text. Therefore, readers could go to specific sections of interest if they desire to do so.

At its heart, the book explores how great organizations (see Chapter 4) try to master the delicate balance between freedom and structure, weaving it into the fabric of their being. This integration needs to be evident in every facet, from organizational culture and the hiring process to the organizational structure itself. Similarly, high-performing teams (see Chapter 5) apply this dynamic interplay in decision-making, project development, and even conducting meetings and brainstorming sessions.

To set the stage for the primary discussions, the book introduces a management framework known as the "Agile Equilibrium," which balances freedom and structure (see Chapter 1). This framework serves as a strategic response to the challenges that organizations encounter, whether they are due to being overly structured (explored in Chapter 2), or excessively free (discussed in Chapter 3).

Organizational
practices
p. 36

Organizing
meetings
p. 76

Organizational
structure
p. 32

STRUCTURE

Organize
brainstorming
sessions
p. 73

Recruitment
p. 28

FREEDOM

Planning projects
p. 70

Company culture
p. 22

Taking decisions
p. 66

Organizational
level

Team
level

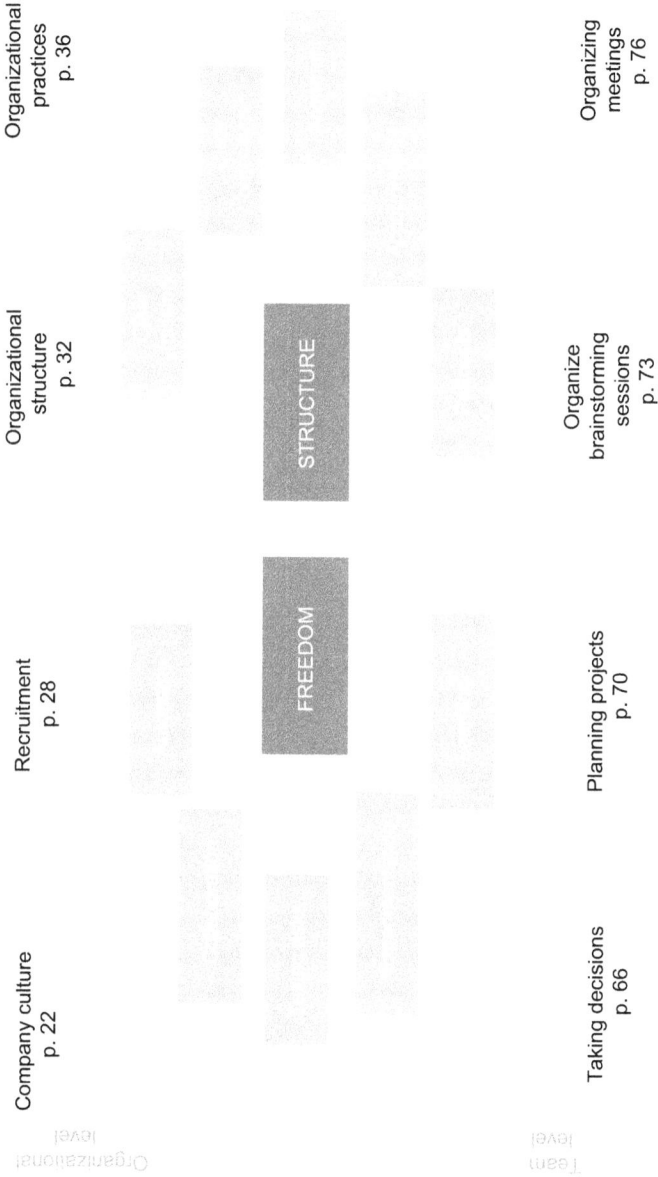

Figure P.1 Structure of the book based on the agile equilibrium

Source: Developed by the author

Acknowledgments

This book is the culmination of an iterative journey, one that has been shaped by countless reflections, readings, dialogues, and exchanges about management in organizations and teams. Many colleagues, friends, and clients have contributed in meaningful ways to its development and finalization.

I would first like to acknowledge the authors whose work has been a source of inspiration throughout my journey. Books such as Jim Collins' *Good to Great,* who greatly inspired the development of the book's framework, and Frederic Laloux's *Reinventing Organizations* have provided invaluable insights into organizational dynamics, leadership, and team performance. Their ideas, alongside those of many others, laid the foundation for much of the thinking in this book.

I am also grateful to Leonid Goncharov, Otu Ekanem, Lucio Campanelli, and Delia Carlesi, with whom I engaged in rich conversations about management and leadership. I have also been deeply inspired by the management styles of Lejla Sadiku and Anne-Lucie Lefebvre, whose approaches to leadership have influenced some ideas in this book.

I had the privilege of discussing and testing several of the book's themes with my students at Sciences Po and Mohammed VI Polytechnic University. Their insights and perspectives helped shape and refine the content significantly.

A special thanks to those who took the time to carefully review and offer feedback on the manuscript. Among others, I would like to thank Mareta Alieva, Bidjan Nashat, Lejla Sadiku, Stefano Mastrogiacomo, Mohammad Sear, Enzo Caputo, Stephanie Wade, and Benjamina Mahasolo Randrianarivelo. Your detailed comments and thoughtful critiques helped improve the clarity and accessibility of the work.

I am also indebted to the members of my Community of Practice, which includes collaborators and former students who contributed to discussions around several dimensions of the book. I am especially thankful to Bilen Barzaghi, Eduardo de la Chica, Karl Fahlvik, and Melanie Skenderi for their support.

A big thank you to Louise Longeau for her work on the illustrations and the book cover, which have brought my ideas to life visually.

Last but certainly not least, I would like to extend my sincere gratitude to my publisher, BEP, for trusting me with this project and for their ongoing support throughout the process. Their efforts in making this book accessible and engaging for a wide audience have been invaluable, and I hope that the ideas presented here resonate with many.

My Story

Early Enthusiasm and Harsh Realities in Big Bureaucracy

When I first joined well-known international organizations, as a junior expert, my enthusiasm was off the charts. For a young person eager to make a positive mark in the world, it seemed like a dream opportunity!

However, reality soon hit home. Despite the enormous potential—a lot of smart people, huge resources at our disposal, you name it—it seemed to me that we often struggled to meet our objectives, and project implementation was riddled with challenges. Over time, I realized that these hurdles weren't always the typical issues faced in development projects due to the complex contexts (think, for instance, about political issues and personnel turnover in the government). Indeed, I sensed that team collaboration in the organizations where I worked was far from being effective or efficient. *A significant part of the problem was, in my view, the way we were working together as teams to develop and implement strategies and projects.* There were frequent issues such as lack of coordination, working in silos, and poor communication, which often led to fragmented efforts and missed opportunities. These challenges hindered, to my appraisal, our ability to align on goals and leverage our collective strengths effectively.

Another major thing that frustrated me was that employees like myself faced many constraints when it came to taking initiatives, or implementing new ideas. During my early years in these organizations, I possessed the kind of enthusiasm and ideas that were common among my peers. Like many young professionals, I believed that my energy and innovative thinking could lead to solutions, whether I was working on a project in Mozambique or in Colombia. I had this notion that I could simply approach my supervisor, share my ideas, and then, if they had any merit, we could promptly test and implement them. However, I soon discovered that my initial optimism had been somewhat naïve. For instance, I recall an incident where, after I spoke at an internal meeting in a large organization, my boss didn't speak to me for several weeks. I later understood that he was displeased because I had spoken without seeking his permission beforehand. *The intricate bureaucracy governing these organizations, characterized by a multitude of rules and protocols, made it challenging to navigate such a straightforward path.*

So, I started asking myself how it was possible to work more effectively and efficiently and started researching how teams and organizations could truly excel. This exploration intensified when I decided to leave one of those international organizations and began collaborating with start-ups and more dynamic organizations.

I embarked on a significant research journey, but as you've probably heard many times, learning by doing often provides the best insights. This is precisely why, after leaving the World Bank, I started collaborating with a couple of start-ups during my time in the United States. Upon my return to Europe, I continued these collaborations, especially with one start-up.

What unfolded within me was a realization that various tools and approaches existed, which allowed teams and organizations to thrive and be more effective despite important constraints, whether they were limited financial resources or tight deadlines. I also realized that when teams are given guidance and clarity, along with enough room to take initiatives, they become happier and more productive. This realization fueled my hope, and I started contemplating ways to facilitate the adoption of these effective approaches in organizations that, we might euphemistically say, were not always hitting their peak performance, especially in the public sector.

The Shift to Dynamic Organizations and the Chaos Within

When working with start-ups, I quickly realized that these smaller, more nimble organizations operated quite differently to the large organizations where I had worked. For instance, they made quicker decisions and had a distinct culture. I had to adapt myself (even in the way I communicated!) as I discovered that I needed to pick up the pace. I clearly remember my discussions with one entrepreneur where I was supposed to update him on the projects I was supervising in just a few minutes, and often had to speak rather quickly, while he was walking to the next meeting!

However, it became apparent to me that these companies often operated with a certain level of 'chaos' or lack of structure. For instance, the company's direction and vision were not always clear, nor were they effectively communicated to all employees. Now, consider what I said earlier about large organizations, where I often found myself frustrated by the myriad rules and protocols, not to mention the lack of freedom. On the flip side, when I was working with start-ups, what struck me was that there was frequently an absence of the kind of structure and clear protocols that could enhance productivity.

I decided to continue my dual journey, working with international organizations and start-ups. Simultaneously, I kept my research efforts focused on exceptionally innovative organizations and their functioning.

It was during this period that I formulated two central research questions:

1. Why do some organizations achieve greatness and peak performance, and what are the key elements that facilitate this?
2. What practices do they develop to help teams work effectively?

I started thinking about how it was possible to nurture organizations and teams that embodied both freedom and structure: the "freedom" for employees to be more empowered and engaged so they could generate, implement ideas, and take initiatives; and the "structure" for employees to be able to have a system in place that clarified the company direction and mission, and provided some "safety" for them.

To further delve into these questions, I developed several courses at a university in Paris. Teaching these courses provided me with a unique opportunity to learn alongside my students; together, we sought to unravel these complex questions. This opportunity to do research and teaching also allowed me to bridge the gap between my research and practical applications.

In every collaborative endeavor, be it with a team from a major corporation or within an academic project, my focus increasingly centered on cultivating high-performing and agile teams, while honing in on the dynamics of how people collaborate effectively despite dealing with uncertainty and complex challenges. I also began advising large organizations on how to become more nimble and agile.

Embracing Agility for Digital Transformation

Agility is now a recurring topic in the headlines and in business literature, and the call for organizations to embrace it is getting louder. This concept—the necessity for organizations and teams to develop working practices that make them more effective and efficient in the face of uncertainty—will be a central focus in this book.

I believe that the growing demand for so-called agile organizations is primarily a response to the breathtaking pace of change in the modern world, particularly in the context of digital transformation. The world is in a constant state of flux, with rapid transformations unfolding around us.

In my course on innovation in the public sector at SciencesPo, I often use a slide in one of the early classes to illustrate why public sector organizations need to embrace innovation. We are dealing with higher citizen expectations, complex and often "wicked" problems,* uncertainties stemming from global crises, and a world driven by the need for speed—which means that the public sector is under increased pressure to deliver quick results (for instance, by delivering better services to citizens who expect the same level of quality from the private sector).

Even if you think outside the public sector, *the present landscape demands a higher level of adaptability and agility from organizations and teams.*

Let's take a moment to consider technology that envelops us nowadays (as I write these lines, I woke up to yet another article about ChatGPT and its potential applications and updates). Technology has had a profound impact on companies, with the lifespan of businesses shrinking dramatically due to increased competition and various factors. Organizations everywhere are clearly striving to integrate technology more effectively.

However, what often happens—drawing on my own experience—is that many digital transformation initiatives face challenges in meeting their objectives. Interestingly, the analysis of these failures often points to management issues rather than technological shortcomings. For instance, when you look at the research around the causes of the significant failure of "healthcare.gov"†—a $1 billion project aimed at developing a digital

---

* A wicked problem is a complex issue with no clear solution, characterized by incomplete, contradictory, and changing requirements, making it difficult to solve.

† The primary objective of Healthcare.gov was to facilitate the enrollment process for Americans seeking health insurance under the Affordable Care Act (ACA). The website aimed to simplify the comparison and purchase of insurance plans and was expected to be a cornerstone of the ACA's goal to expand health care access to millions of uninsured Americans. However, when Healthcare.gov launched in October 2013, the system was unable to handle the volume of users trying to register and browse health insurance plans. The site crashed repeatedly, plagued by an array of technical issues such as server overloads, coding errors, and functionality flaws in the user interface. These problems prevented many users from registering for health insurance, leading to widespread criticism and putting significant political pressure on the administration to quickly resolve the issues. The failure of the website at launch was a stark illustration of the challenges in deploying large-scale public sector IT projects without sufficient testing, iterative development, and system flexibility. Initially, the project was indeed managed

platform to help people choose and subscribe to health insurance—you will see that considerable part of the project's problems stemmed from inflexible procurement processes and insufficient platform testing—a lack of "freedom," if I may refer back to my earlier comments.

With the same token, research shows that Nokia's failure to evolve its technology and remain competitive, despite being the best-selling phone manufacturer in 1992 (in contrast to its decline, which meant that, by 2007, it was accounting for only 50 percent of cell phones sold due to iPhone's growing share of the market), was also linked to organizational issues. Among these was a culture of fear within the organization, where middle managers hesitated to speak truthfully due to the fear of termination, and senior managers felt intimidated by middle managers, and thus accused them of lacking ambition to achieve goals.[1]

Another example is the research conducted by Columbia University on the underlying problems that led to the NASA Challenger accident in 1986. These were also related to the culture of the organization and management practices—even though some engineers and managers within the company saw evidence that something was wrong when preparing for the Challenger mission, they carried on as if nothing was wrong as they were afraid to speak-up.[2] These examples illuminate an important lesson: the challenges faced in both cases were rooted less in technological shortcomings and more in the absence of a culture that fostered innovation and empowered employees with a clear sense of mission and vision.

This realization brings to the forefront the concept that *agility is essential not just for operational improvement but also as a cornerstone of digital transformation.*

Indeed, in my work developing workshops and courses on digital transformation, I consistently emphasize the importance of integrating agility into the digital transformation narrative. After all, digital

---

using a traditional "waterfall" approach, which is linear and sequential, relying heavily on getting each stage right the first time without much room for revising based on ongoing feedback. This method proved inadequate for a complex, large-scale IT project that required adaptability in the face of evolving requirements and unexpected technical challenges.

transformation is about rethinking and reimagining how an organization conducts its business by leveraging emerging technologies.

Now, I strongly believe that organizations across all sectors need to embrace agility and nimbleness, and that this need has only intensified with the acceleration of rapid technological advancements.

Consider, for instance, a government official in the Ministry of Education tasked with developing a learning platform to enhance interactions between students and professors. Success in such endeavors hinges on the ability to engage with beneficiaries, iteratively test and refine the platform based on user feedback, collaborate across departments, and foster teamwork among colleagues.

Experts worldwide consistently highlight the exponential pace of technological growth, which is at a pace that many organizations struggle to keep up. Despite the technological leaps we have witnessed, the productivity and development models of many organizations remain anchored in the industrial age. In its blurb, the book *Exponential* by Azeem Azhar ask the reader to consider "how technology is leaving us behind and what to do about it."[3] What does this mean? It means that organizations and teams need to adopt better and more flexible ways of working in order to integrate emerging technologies and, as mentioned earlier, respond to today's complex challenges.

"It's All About Management"

It's essential to recognize that the path to innovation and digital transformation is not merely about adopting new technologies. Instead, it's about fostering a culture that encourages innovation, empowers employees, and embraces the principles of agility as fundamental to navigating the complexities and opportunities of the digital age.

To me, this is first a matter of creating and developing great organizations and performing teams—so "it's all about management."

As we have seen from the examples of big organizations struggling with digital transformation, poor management practices—specifically how organizations and teams operate—emerged as a significant issue.

Similarly, management is and should remain a crucial element for start-ups, echoing the sentiments of start-up guru, Eric Ries, who emphasizes that *"entrepreneurship essentially encompasses management."*[4] From my observations, start-ups lacking high-performing teams that are adept at executing and implementing ideas seldom achieve long-term success. The essence of an effective start-up lies not merely in ideation, which is comparatively straightforward, but in a team's ability to operationalize these ideas effectively and efficiently—this is also about the way founders manage the company. This transition from concept to reality is where the true challenge lies, underscoring the indispensable value of robust management practices within the start-up ecosystem.

Simplifying Complexity in Management

If we agree that management is such an important concept, then why is it often misunderstood or underutilized?

My frustration with the management practices I encountered was not limited to traditional organizations or start-ups; it extended across both realms.

My observation is that even fundamental management concepts, such as motivating people, providing clear direction, and ensuring effective communication, often seemed unfamiliar to or were not effectively utilized by many of the managers I encountered. It was surprising to me because one would expect managers to possess a solid grasp of these principles! Unfortunately, in many cases, there was a noticeable absence of adequate management training. As a side note, I firmly believe that you don't need to attend Harvard Business School to comprehend these fundamental management principles and best practices. Learning by doing and applying these concepts can be equally effective.

While it is true that there is already a plethora of management books available today sharing valuable insights and practices, I feel that a significant portion of them tends to be densely written and complex. This complexity may partly explain why many managers, despite their importance, may not delve into these books as often as they should.

This leads me to one of the factors behind my decision to write this book: *the idea of simplifying complexity.* Bear with me for a moment—it never ceases to amaze me how some individuals dismiss concepts like "agility" as being too intricate and unattainable for their organizations. What I want to show is that agility, like other management concepts, must

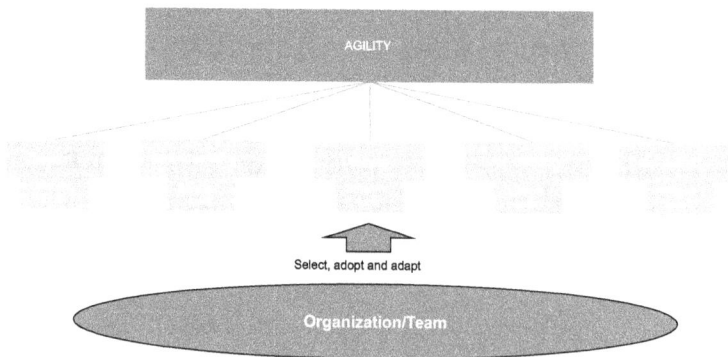

Figure M.1 *Unpacking agility*

Source: Developed by the author

be broken down and understood step by step. What I would emphasize is the need to unpack agility, highlighting its underlying principles, such as iteration and citizen-centricity, and showcasing practical approaches that can be tailored to specific organizational contexts (Figure M.1).

This is exactly what I'd like to do here—to showcase some good practices, examples, and tools that help build the kind of structure and freedom *that organizations and teams can adopt and adapt to their specific contexts.*

In this book, I will show those good practices *through a straightforward framework—the agile equilibrium—which focuses on management.* This lens can help simplify complexity, considering both the structural and innovative aspects of these practices.

I hope that readers, including managers, will find inspiration in the practices we discuss and will be encouraged to conduct further research and potentially implement some of these ideas.

Empowering Employees: A Path to Happiness at Work

Another reason why I embarked on this journey to write about the subject was my observation of a substantial number of friends and acquaintances employed by various companies, in both the private and public sectors, who seemed deeply frustrated and unhappy at work.

Through conversations with them, *I realized that their discontent wasn't primarily about the volume of work; instead, it was centered on the way teams functioned within their organizations.* Issues such as micromanagement, a lack of freedom, and unclear alignment or contribution played a significant role. These are topics we will delve into in our conversation.

If you agree with me then, in a way, this book is also about happiness at work and the imperative to "humanize" organizations. As Frederic Laloux eloquently asks in his book, "can we create soulful workplaces where our talents can flourish, and our callings can be honored?"[5]

When you consider the amount of time we spend at work (let's say an average of 70 to 80 percent of our day), it becomes evident that our work experiences significantly impact our lives. So, why not strive to create more pleasant and exciting workplaces? That's one of the key themes we'll explore—how to develop organizations that can provide some structure and overall direction but can, at the same time, truly give responsibilities to employees, and thus empower them.

This reminds me of a simple yet highly interesting diagram showing a pyramid (loosely based on Maslow's hierarchy of needs) that I came across in the book "Peak" by the current Airbnb adviser and founder of Joie de Vivre Hotel, Chip Conley (Figure M.2).[6]

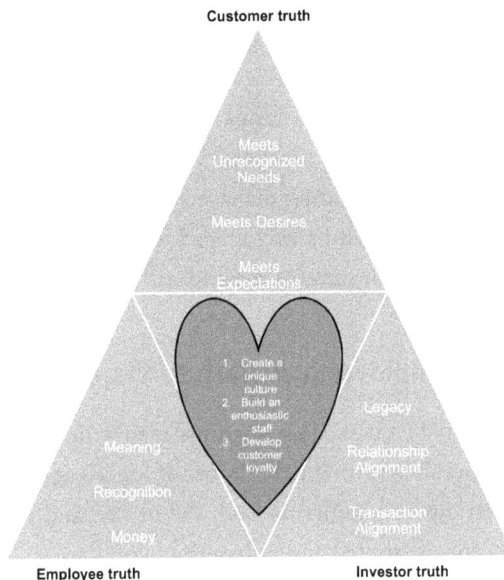

Figure M.2 Empowering employees[7]

Adapted from Chip Conley's book, Peak

The pyramid shows that companies should primarily focus on their employees and contribute to their self-fulfillment. When employees are happy and productive, they, in turn, will make customers happy. If customers are also content, they will be more inclined to use the company's services or products. Ultimately, this cycle leads to investor satisfaction. So, what is the bottom line? The bottom line is that the key to achieving higher productivity and better results is to invest in your employees and company culture.

Regrettably, this principle is often not realized in practice. I often meet people working across a variety of sectors—from development to luxury—who are overwhelmed by stress and disengaged from their work. This disengagement often leads to burnout, which, in my view, is less about the volume of work and more about a lack of alignment and a sense of purpose in their roles. In its 2022 State of the Global Workplace report, Gallup revealed alarming levels of worker disengagement and unhappiness. The findings show that 60 percent of employees feel emotionally detached at work, and 19 percent describe themselves as miserable. Additionally, only 33 percent of workers report feeling engaged, a decline from the figure reported in 2020.[8]

It's crucial to emphasize that I'm not suggesting that the cause lies solely with specific people within these organizations. What I am suggesting is that the problem of poor management stems from deficient management systems, rather than individual shortcomings.

Let me provide an example. A friend of mine recently lamented his unfortunate experience with two different managers in one organization. Manager X engaged in excessive micromanagement, resulting in a lack of motivation for effective work. On the other hand, Manager Y failed to provide clear responsibilities or adequate supervision, so my friend didn't have any incentives to reward high productivity. When I inquired about his experience, he attributed it to "bad luck in encountering individuals who lack the necessary managerial skills."

By contrast, I don't attribute this to chance. I believe it's not solely the fault of these two "bad" managers; it is more likely to be an issue inherent in the organization itself—a lack of a strong organizational culture, practices, and values that incentivize employees and managers to work more effectively.

Therefore, the solution for this particular situation would not be to replace those two managers, but to create an organizational environment that empowers employees while establishing a robust and supportive structure for them.

The Ideal Reader: A Curious Manager

As we touched on earlier, there's a widespread management issue in many of the organizations I've been part of and studied. One key problem is that individuals who transition into managerial roles often lack the training in innovative management approaches they need to effectively lead and develop teams. Moreover, many management books can be too complex for the average reader.

What I want to accomplish with this book is to share the knowledge I've gained from my experiences and research, making it accessible to a wider audience. I believe that this book will be valuable for managers in both large organizations and start-ups, as well as students who aspire to become managers in the future. By addressing the needs of both current and future managers, I aim to cultivate a deeper understanding of effective management practices.

My hope is that it will help them understand and implement better management practices, ultimately leading to more effective and happier workplaces.

Conclusion

Joining esteemed institutions such as the United Nations and the World Bank filled me with immense enthusiasm and a desire to make a significant impact. However, I quickly encountered the harsh realities of large bureaucracies. Despite the abundance of smart individuals and vast resources, achieving our objectives often felt like an uphill battle, plagued by ineffective team collaboration and a restrictive environment that stifled innovation and initiative.

This realization propelled me on a quest to discover how teams and organizations could excel despite these constraints. My journey took me from large international organizations to dynamic start-ups, where I observed the stark contrast in decision-making speed and organizational culture. Yet, these smaller entities often struggled with a lack of structure and clear direction, highlighting the need for a balance between freedom and structure.

The insights I gained through this exploration, supported by research and hands-on experience, led me to formulate two central questions: what makes some organizations great, and how do they build high-performing teams? This book aims to bring more clarity around these questions by offering practical strategies and tools to foster agile, empowered, and efficient teams and organizations. It will do so by introducing a framework to help readers navigate the complexity of the subject (see next).

CHAPTER 1

Introducing the Agile Equilibrium Framework

Balancing Freedom and Structure in Management

As I mentioned earlier, whether I was working in the public sector, private sector, or academic sector, I began to identify some crucial elements of teams and organizational performance. On one hand, I observed that teams (organizations) perform exceptionally well when they are empowered and have the flexibility to develop, test, and implement ideas—this is what I would often observe in start-ups. At the same time, I noticed that teams can only thrive when there is a clear structure in place, with well-defined roles, responsibilities, and a common direction to follow. This is what I often saw in well-established complex organizations.

These are the two fundamental dimensions of the management framework I would like to present here—freedom and structure. At first glance, when considering organizational and team performance, they may appear to be in conflict with each other. However, they are not.

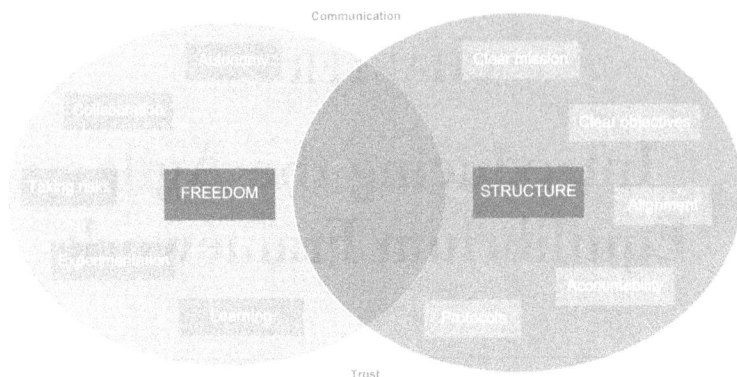

Figure 1.1 The Agile Equilibrium Framework

Source: Developed by the author

What I'm suggesting is that, for organizations and teams to perform at their best, they need to strike a balance between these two dimensions.

The Agile Equilibrium Framework

As I delved into Jim Collins' seminal work, *Good to Great*,[1] I found myself captivated by the matrix of "creative discipline" he introduced. It offered an insightful perspective—a kind of framework through which I could grasp the intricate world of management.

Inspired by this framework, I took it upon myself to develop a slightly modified version based on my personal experiences and research. *I sought to create a more comprehensible model that could be easily understood by a broader audience—a model showing the agile equilibrium that organizations and teams need to strike to achieve peak performance.*

As illustrated in Figure 1.1, the Agile Equilibrium Framework represents the balance between structure and freedom that high-performing organizations and teams strive to achieve.

Structure

1. Clear and Well-Defined Mission: This is about developing a mission that not only outlines the organization's purpose but also resonates with and motivates employees. Ideally, the mission should be inspirational and provide a clear direction for all organizational activities.
2. Clearly Defined and Measurable Objectives: It is important to make objectives measurable and time-bound (to facilitate clear understanding and tracking of progress).
3. Alignment: Individual and team goals need to be aligned with the overall mission and objectives of the organization. This could include strategies for regularly reviewing and adjusting objectives to maintain alignment in a changing environment.
4. Clear Accountability Structure: There is a need for transparent roles and responsibilities within teams, to prevent overlaps and gaps in task ownership.
5. Standardized Protocols: Standardized processes play an important role in ensuring efficiency and consistency in working on projects. These processes need to be designed to allow for flexibility and adaptability where necessary.

Freedom

1. Autonomy: This is not only about giving responsibilities but also providing the necessary resources and authority to make decisions. It is also about allowing individuals and teams to have control over their work processes and schedules, in order to foster a sense of ownership and engagement.
2. Collaboration: Cross-functional teams and diverse perspectives can play a major role in enhancing creativity and problem-solving.

3. Calculated Risk-Taking: Risks need to be assessed and managed rather than anyone being reckless; creating a supportive environment where failure is seen as a learning opportunity could also be beneficial.
4. Experimentation: There is often a need for quick, iterative testing of ideas to innovate and adapt faster.
5. Learning: It is also important to commit to continuous learning to be able to constantly improve.

On one side of this equilibrium, we have "structure," which is characterized by a clear and well-defined mission, precisely delineated objectives, and a robust alignment across all levels of the organization. This structure needs to be supported by a transparent team and accountability framework. These elements of "structure" work in concert to provide a stable foundation upon which the dynamic and experimental activities encapsulated by the dimension of "freedom" can thrive: autonomy, collaboration, risk-taking, experimentation, and learning. This framework hinges on two fundamental conditions: effective communication and deep-seated trust. I'll delve deeper into this later.

Harnessing Chaos With Structure—Finding the Right Balance

Together, these dimensions form the bedrock of a framework designed to empower organizations to achieve their missions while fostering a culture of innovation and continuous improvement and for teams to achieve their objectives effectively and efficiently. Organizations and teams need to strike a balance between these two "extremes."

Consider, for instance, a recent book coauthored by the founder of Netflix titled *No Rules Rules.*[2] This book implicitly emphasizes the importance of having some rules and structure while allowing employees in the company the freedom to take initiative, and empowering them to do so. *No Rules Rules* delves into Netflix's unique culture of "Freedom and Responsibility," where employees are given significant autonomy to make decisions, alongside clearly defined expectations for responsibility. This approach is exemplified by their policy of not tracking vacation days, which empowers employees to take time off at their discretion, provided they meet their professional goals and contribute positively to the team's success.

The same principle applies to various other innovative and great organizations I came across, which we will discuss shortly.

It is important to understand that leaning too far in either direction isn't conducive to either team or organizational performance.

To draw an analogy, *we can consider the tension and complementarity between analytical thinking and intuitive thinking*.

Let me clarify this.

You may be familiar with the concept of design thinking, which is a widely known process that teams and organizations can use to understand users' needs, challenge assumptions, redefine problems, and create innovative solutions to prototype and test.

Now, design thinking blends analytical thinking with intuitive intuition, as the whole process involves a dynamic interplay between these two thinking methods. This starts with trying to collect data and identify patterns to understand users' needs (which is more analytical), but moves on to brainstorming possible ideas and solutions to address those needs (which is more intuitive). What I am implying here is that this process should not bend too much in either direction.

The same applies to the framework I am presenting for freedom and structure—organizations or teams should find a balance between those two dimensions, and this is essential for innovation.

Applying the Agile Equilibrium Framework

Whether I'm building a team or have been asked to advise organizations on how to enhance their performance and become more agile, I always consider striking a balance between the two dimensions we just discussed. For instance, in Tunisia, I was working on an innovative project, and I spent quite some time developing a team that had not only enough "freedom" to innovate and take initiative but also enough "structure" to clarify who was doing what and when. Likewise, when advising a start-up, I also spent some time discussing with the founder how to develop an innovative culture that allowed people to be empowered (freedom), but at the same time to develop a mission and alignment between the employees (structure). We will be discussing those examples at length later on.

What is interesting is that, even on my own (individual level), I structure my time and tasks by thinking about how to define a process that is not only sufficiently structured but also allows me to have some freedom—we will discuss this subject later.

In a way, *this lens serves me as a constant reminder of the perpetual need to find a balance between these two dimensions*, whatever the project I am working on. It's the recognition that too much of one aspect or the other can hinder progress.

Conclusion

As I explored different sectors—public, private, and academic—I began to recognize key elements that drive team and organizational performance. In start-ups, I observed that flexibility and empowerment allowed teams to innovate and implement ideas effectively. Conversely, well-established organizations thrived on clear structure, well-defined roles, responsibilities, and a unified direction.

These experiences led me to understand that high-performing teams and organizations must strike a balance between freedom and structure. Initially, these dimensions may seem contradictory, but they are, in fact, complementary. The concept of agile equilibrium embodies this balance, enabling organizations and teams to thrive by maintaining flexibility within a structured framework. This approach not only enhances operational efficiency but also fosters innovation and continuous improvement, providing a roadmap for sustainable success.

Before seeing how this framework can be applied in practice, it is important though to consider the perils for organizations and teams of leaning toward too much structure or too much freedom. Let's start with the former (see next).

CHAPTER 2

The Challenges of Excessive Structure

Defining Traditional Organizations as Command and Control Structures

It is important to recognize the pivotal role of organizations—they are indeed fundamental for us if we want to collaborate and create solutions to complex problems, whether in agriculture, health care, or any other sector. Organizations have been the cornerstone of human progress, enabling us to pool resources, share knowledge, and coordinate efforts on a scale that would be impossible individually. In *Reinventing Organizations*,[1] Frederic Laloux aptly notes that nearly all human advances throughout history have been a result of organizational collaboration.

However, as we were discussing earlier, *many organizations today still maintain a traditional approach in their operations*. These entities have not adapted their work methodologies, processes, or cultural frameworks to the ever-evolving landscape. They persist in employing the same tools and approaches, adhering to conventional structures that were set up to address the Industrial Revolution challenges 100 years ago!

I like Seth Godin's analogy in *Tribes*,[2] likening modern corporations to a royal setup whereby a CEO acts as a monarch around whom the organization is structured like a kingdom.

Traditional organizations often operate as "command-and-control" structures, relying heavily on directives, control, and sanctions. This approach, rooted in the Taylorian model and the "waterfall" methodology, effectively applied Adam Smith's principles of division of labor during the Industrial Revolution. In this model, tasks are broken down into repetitive, predictable components, optimizing efficiency for mass production. This structure ensures clear lines of authority and responsibility, making it suitable for environments where consistency and uniformity are paramount.

However, traditional organizations, which thrived under predictable and stable conditions, are much less effective in today's world, characterized by complexity and uncertainty. As we discussed earlier, traditional organizations with an abundance of rules and procedures have difficulty addressing problems that are increasingly more complex, and that demand a much higher level of adaptability and flexibility in the decision-making process.

This issue was clearly articulated in an article by McKinsey[3]: "Simply put, the dominant traditional organizational model evolved primarily for stability in a well-known environment; it assumes that the world is predictable. It is based on the idea of an organization as a machine, and tends to favor a static, siloed, structural hierarchy ... However, as the world grows more complex, this view gives rise to further matrix-like structure, and more rules ... When Nokia, Eastman Kodak, and Motorola, which had once been feted as icons of management and innovation, lost their way, it was not because they weren't smart, but because their organizations were designed for a world that was rapidly disappearing."

The Perils of Overly Detailed Planning in Traditional Organizations: Personal Examples

Let me tell you about three experiences I had in the past. We will then try to distill some of the cross-cutting problems and obstacles in those situations.

I was involved in a project with an international organization focused on developing a public sector reform project in Mozambique. It was a significant endeavor, particularly in a developing country, considering the various contextual factors, approaches, and stakeholders. During the project development phase, I began to question our extensive eight-month planning process. Our project document, indeed, required a precise, detailed layout of all activities for the upcoming five years, directly linked to the budget. Moreover, the multiple layers of approval and review in the organization prolonged the project development or revision processes. In a context as dynamic as Mozambique, where circumstances often undergo rapid changes, such as government turnover, I found myself wondering about the necessity and feasibility of such precise planning. When I approached my manager about this, I was told that the organization had a strong aversion to uncertainty and preferred meticulously planned strategies, to avoid any unknowns. As anticipated, during the project implementation phase, the government turnover changed hands, and the new ministry representative didn't validate several of the meticulously planned activities. This required a revision of the project document, which proved to be a cumbersome and time-consuming process. Revising the document involved respecifying both new and previously planned activities, leading to significant delays and frustration.

This experience left me puzzled. *The need for such detailed planning, especially when the implementation of activities over several years was uncertain, seemed counterproductive.* This extensive planning led to frustration, not just within our team but also from our client, the Mozambican government, due to our lack of responsiveness and the prolonged development period. The delays in the progress became evident when another organization swiftly initiated a similar project, while we were still finalizing ours, and by then, our project had become redundant.

In Tunisia, I recall a situation where I convinced a team leader in an international organization to adopt innovative design thinking approaches for a digital transformation program in North Africa, funded by the organization I was associated with. However, my excitement soon turned to frustration when the same person contacted me to tell that *our plans—focused on testing and experimenting—were simply not feasible due to the organization's rigid procurement process.* This inflexibility meant that unexpected activities were not tolerated, and every aspect of the project had to be meticulously predetermined and financially secured.

Similarly, in Madagascar, while working on a compelling public sector project for an international organization, the team leader and I believed that, in order to develop a knowledge management platform, we needed to explore options other than conventional outsourcing. We were searching for innovative solutions. With this in mind, we saw the potential for innovative companies, particularly start-ups, to contribute significantly to the project. We actively spread the word to encourage their involvement. However, *during the bidding process, due to technical requirements and stringent protocols within the procurement system, many of the innovative companies and start-ups that had applied—some with compelling ideas for the platform's development—fell short of meeting the strict criteria,* hindering their participation in the project.

Common Obstacles in Traditional Organizations

These examples hint at some of the constraints of traditional organizations, such as overplanning (because, as human beings, we are quite bad at planning ...), getting stuck in a constant analysis process, decisions from the top, rigid processes and protocols, and a lack of employee empowerment. In traditional organizations, it is in fact common to see:

- Top management setting the objectives;
- Decisions on how to do things also being set by the top management;

- A control system being imposed to ensure compliance.

The abovementioned three stories demonstrate that this is not an effective or efficient approach to work and to do innovation.

The Fear Factor in Traditional Organizations

I want to highlight another significant issue I've encountered firsthand in traditional organizations.

To do so, let me share a story about a recent meeting within an organization I was working with (to provide some context, I was part of a team responsible for developing a toolkit designed to spread innovation across various teams within the organization). The meeting lacked a clear agenda and objectives, which was the first noticeable issue. There was also a senior official present who had not taken the time to familiarize themselves with the toolkit we had been developing for nearly a year, despite the impending deadline.

During the meeting, this senior official, being the most senior figure present, took the reins and proposed a significant restructuring of the document. While some of the suggestions had merit, the official did not have a comprehensive understanding of the context, having not reviewed the document. This led to palpable frustration within the team. However, as often happens in such settings, no one felt empowered to question or defend our approach. There seemed to be an inherent reluctance to express dissent or articulate a differing opinion.

What this scenario highlights is *the prevalence of a kind of defer-ence and conformity within traditional organizations, what I would term as "organizational fear,"* subordinates feel inhibited from criticizing or expressing strong dissenting opinions to their superiors.[*]

In observing leadership dynamics within traditional organizations, the TV series *Succession*[†] offers a vivid portrayal of autocratic

---

[*] This discussion of deference and conformity within traditional organizations touches on fundamental issues such as incentive structures and power dynamics. These topics are explored in depth in other scholarly works and are beyond the detailed scope of this book, even though they are crucial for understanding the underlying mechanisms of "organizational fear."

[†] *Succession*, HBO, first aired 2018.

decision-making and its impact on corporate culture. The depiction of the company founder making unilateral decisions that are enforced by employees, who exhibit a significant fear of objecting or expressing dissent, seems eerily reflective of the environments we often encounter.

The Negative Impact of Excessive Structure on Employee Motivation and Productivity

The example I just provided may seem a bit exaggerated, as the reality is often more nuanced and complex. However, my aim here is to highlight some major obstacles faced by traditional organizations that negatively impact employees' motivation and hamper the development of a truly motivating work environment.

Reflecting on one of my early roles in an international organization, I recall feeling somewhat marginalized; it felt like I was being perceived as a person with too many ideas who took the initiative too frequently. On one occasion, my boss expressed displeasure because, during an internal team meeting, I volunteered to present our project without seeking individual permission beforehand. I saw it as an effort to be helpful, but my boss felt differently.

My overarching sentiment was that I struggled to align with many of the organizations where I worked because I couldn't fully express my real self—someone who enjoys taking initiative, being helpful, and developing and implementing ideas. In the book *Reinventing Organizations*, Frédéric Laloux *identifies a major problem in traditional organizations as being the lack of "wholeness."* The concept of "wholeness" refers to the need to create work environments where people can bring their full selves to work, integrating their personal and professional lives in a way that fosters authenticity and complete participation. When this doesn't happen, it stifles creativity and engagement, leading to workplaces where people feel they must hide parts of themselves, which can, in turn, decrease satisfaction and productivity.

If you look at the research on employee engagement, you will see that it suggests that people perform better when they're motivated and, as Laloux indicated, when they can express themselves.

Research also shows that employees are better motivated when they fulfill three dimensions: mastery; purpose; and autonomy.[5] According to Daniel Pink, the strongest motivation is intrinsic; what motivates people is for them to be able to: thoroughly know the subject they are working on; to understand how they are contributing to the overall mission of the company; and to have the opportunity to have some autonomy when it comes to how they implement the things they are supposed to do.

Now, this does not often happen in *traditional organizations; people in them mostly lack "autonomy" as there are too many rules and protocols that hamper people's willingness and ability to take initiative.* And when you do that, you hamper innovation and creativity. As former CEO of 3M, William L. McKnight, put it well: "If you put a fence around people at work you get sheep."

Conclusion

Many organizations (and teams within) cling to traditional approaches, failing to adapt their methodologies, processes, and cultures to the evolving landscape. They persist in using outdated tools and maintaining rigid structures that date back to the industrial revolution.

Traditional organizations often operate under a "command-and-control" model, characterized by top-down directives, rigid control, and a plethora of rules and procedures. This approach, rooted in the Taylorian model and the principles of the industrial revolution, may have been effective in stable, predictable environments, but proves inadequate in today's complex and uncertain world. The rigidity of these structures hampers their ability to respond swiftly to changes and stifles innovation. This chapter has highlighted the significant challenges and inefficiencies inherent in excessive structure, from overplanning and bureaucratic delays to a pervasive fear of taking initiative, all of which can demotivate employees and hinder organizational performance.

On the other side of the equilibrium, leaning toward too much freedom could be problematic for organizations and teams (see next).

CHAPTER 3

The Challenges of Excessive Freedom

Headers

- Defining Start-Ups in Today's Context—15
- Transitioning to the Start-Up Environment: A Case of Empowerment and Agility—16
- The Perils of Excessive Freedom in Start-Up Organizations: Personal Examples—17
- "People Need Some Structure to Feel Safe" —18
- Conclusion—19

Defining Start-Ups in Today's Context

In the context of our discussions, a start-up is an early-stage company striving to deliver a product or service amid a set of constraints and uncertainty.[*] It's important to note that, by start-ups, we refer to companies in their initial phases rather than entities that began small and have evolved into well-established corporations (such as Google). Although these companies may aim to retain some of the characteristics associated with early-stage companies, some have matured, adopting

---

[*] Start-ups are typically defined as early-stage companies engaged in the development and initial delivery of innovative products or services. These organizations operate under significant constraints, including limited resources, uncertain market conditions, and the need for rapid scalability. The nature of start-ups demands high adaptability and resilience as they navigate the complexities and volatility of establishing a new business in competitive environments.

more structured and sophisticated practices, which I'll refer to as "great organizations" shortly.

Transitioning to the Start-Up Environment: A Case of Empowerment and Agility

I have had the opportunity to work with several start-ups, mainly as an adviser in the United States and also within a Paris-based start-up for a number of years. During this time, I engaged with numerous entrepreneurs and had the chance to learn innovative tools and approaches that drive productivity and innovation. In addition, I closely observed how entrepreneurs and start-up founders developed their respective companies, vision, culture, and so on. Remember the question I formulated for my research? How can we build great organizations and great teams? Indeed, my interest has always been to understand how to construct great companies and effective, efficient teams that not only achieve their goals but also inspire and motivate employees.

I found that one of the most fascinating elements of working with start-ups was the pervasive sense of excitement that circulated within these organizations. There was indeed a palpable enthusiasm among the teams, as they came together to create innovative products or services, despite having limited time and resources.

You see, the environment within start-ups is distinctly different from that of traditional organizations—*I could often feel a sense of empowerment and responsibility among the employees that I had never felt when working in traditional organizations.*

In start-ups, there's an overall need to operate with greater speed and agility, and this permeates the whole organization.

Let me illustrate this with an example. In one experience working for a start-up, my role involved developing both virtual and physical communities around the company. This entailed organizing events where people could meet, utilizing digital tools for engagement, and creating a community that seamlessly blended the online and offline spheres. Drawing from my past experiences in corporate environments, my initial instinct was to meticulously craft a detailed plan, complete with a comprehensive list of activities and budget breakdowns.

However, when I presented this elaborate plan to the CEO, hoping for validation, his response was quite the opposite. He looked at me and remarked, "Tommaso, this is too corporate. We don't need such an articulated plan. Our budget is limited, and the landscape is uncertain. What's crucial is not spending excessive time on planning, but instead, being highly reactive to changing circumstances during the implementation." I had a similar reaction when I was looking for validation during the implementation of several other activities.

You can see the stark difference between this and my earlier experiences with the more rigid structures of traditional organizations with rigid procedures and layers of approval.

The Perils of Excessive Freedom in Start-Up Organizations: Personal Examples

Overall, I enjoyed my time working for start-ups, but I did observe a distinct set of challenges—quite different from those observed in traditional organizations. While traditional organizations are laden with extensive structures, rules, and protocols, which often impede innovation, start-ups inherently embody a sense of "freedom"—it is in their DNA. Yet, sometimes those *start-up organizations have far too much freedom, especially at in the early stages, and they lack a well-developed structure around their employees.*

Let me give you an example.

I recall my time working in a start-up in Paris, collaborating on a business development initiative with colleagues. The standout aspect here was the CEO's practice of enabling us (the employees) to determine how to develop and execute activities. This was in contrast to the traditional organizational structure, where decisions on both the "what" and the "how" were often centralized at the managerial level.

However, what I noticed during this project was a degree of redundant effort among my colleagues (as some were working on similar activities and duplicating efforts), resulting, I thought, from a lack of clearly defined responsibilities. There was also a notable discrepancy in alignment with the marketing strategy, raising questions about the coherence and coordination of our efforts.

Referring back to the agile equilibrium, I observed a "lack of structure": an absence of explicit guidance on the mission of the company; how each department and team (in this case, the business development and marketing one) contributed to ultimate vision and mission; who was doing what, and so on.

Another notable experience occurred during my advisory role at a U.S. start-up, where the CEO, a visionary with boundless ideas, often shifted the company's direction and product offerings. His innovative drive was commendable, yet his reluctance to delegate and specify clear roles led to confusion among team members. This constant change not only strained resources but also made it difficult for the team to maintain a focused strategy.

The CEO's approach, while initially allowing for a high degree of flexibility and quick pivots, ultimately resulted in a chaotic work environment. This was exemplified when he announced a sudden shift in product strategy during a critical development phase, without providing a structured plan or clear objectives. The team were talented and adaptable, but they found themselves repeatedly scrambling to realign their work with his changing visions, leading to frustration and inefficiency.

This lack of structure not only affected internal operations but also the start-up's ability to present a cohesive brand to investors and customers. Each change in direction required a realignment of marketing strategies and product development plans, costing valuable time and resources.

"People Need Some Structure to Feel Safe"

Earlier we mentioned that "if you put a fence around people you get sheep." At the same time, you need to have some structure and clear protocols—otherwise, you get teams not having a clear mission or clear responsibilities as in the example I just gave you from the start-up in France.

Richard Sheridan (founder of Menlo Innovations and author of *Joy. inc*) says that *"people need some structure to feel safe."* I agree, and believe that this is somehow related to clarity—clarity about what is expected from the employees, what the vision of the company is, what the practices in the company are, and so on.

As we discussed earlier, building a performing team or organization is about finding the right mix of freedom and structure. Instead of fencing people in, you need to provide them with wide yet clear "boundaries" that guide their actions and keep them aligned with the organization's goals, allowing them to innovate without losing direction.

Conclusion

Working with several start-ups in the United States and Paris revealed the dynamic, innovative atmosphere where employees feel empowered and responsible. However, this environment often suffers from a lack of necessary structure, leading to inefficiencies and confusion. In one start-up, for instance, the absence of clear responsibilities caused redundant efforts and misalignment with the overall strategy.

Excessive freedom without structure can result in a lack of coherent direction. People need some structure to feel safe and clear about expectations and company vision. The challenge for start-ups is to balance freedom with enough structure to provide clarity and direction while maintaining the agility and empowerment that drive innovation.

Having discussed the perils of too much structure and too much freedom, it is now the time to see how the agile equilibrium between freedom and structure can be effectively applied at organizational level (see next).

CHAPTER 4

The Agile Equilibrium at the Organizational Level

Defining Great Organizations

Whether I was immersing myself in reading books about Google, Pixar, Netflix (and talking to the people working there), or about other companies achieving remarkable results in terms of user satisfaction, retention, and profitability, a common thread seemed to emerge—these organizations actively seek an equilibrium between freedom and structure—an agile equilibrium.

I was recently comparing the great companies mentioned in two well-respected management books I had recently read (*Reinventing Organizations* by Frédéric Laloux I just mentioned and *Freedom.inc* by Isaac Getz[1]) and, again, I could see those two dimensions coexisting in the companies the authors mentioned as good examples.

I would like to highlight here that a closer examination of *Freedom.inc*, which seems to overemphasize freedom, reveals that the majority of the companies featured in the book emphasize empowering employees and fostering innovation within a structured context and established rules—indeed the author of this book introduces the concept of "disciplined freedom."[2]

A great organization, in my view, can be defined as one that *consistently finds and maintains a balance between freedom and structure, integrating this equilibrium into every aspect of its DNA.*

As shown in Figure 4.1 this balance is reflected in how great companies embed such approaches into their organizational culture, hiring processes, structure, and organizational practices. Let's examine how these companies strive to achieve this equilibrium to drive performance and innovation.

The Power of Organizational Culture

Company culture, I believe, is one of the most fundamental aspects of a company—it is possibly the main "building block" of a company.

Let's take a moment to consider the emphasis placed by leaders like Satya Nadella, CEO of Microsoft, who prioritized company culture

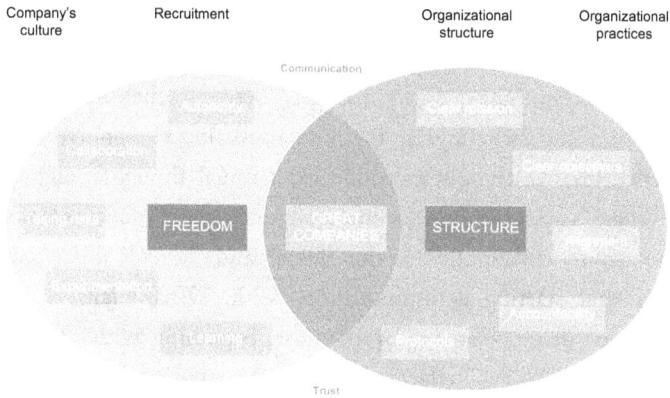

Figure 4.1 Great companies
Source: Developed by the author

upon assuming his role. Nadella eloquently expresses this by saying that the "C" in CEO stands for culture.[3] According to him, the CEO's primary responsibility is to cultivate a culture characterized by listening, learning, and channeling individual passions and talents to support the company's mission. Nadella therefore stresses the importance of a dynamic learning culture with a growth mindset, stating that the goal is to inspire people, rather than merely manage them.

We can refer here to Peter Drucker's famous statement: "culture eats strategy for breakfast," which resonates deeply with the observations we have just made. Organizational culture serves as the bedrock upon which a company is built, wielding significant influence over performance.

Simon Sinek, whose TED talk is one of the most viewed ever, has also underscored the critical role of company culture. For instance, in his book *Start with Why*,[4] he mentions how Apple focuses on creating a culture where employees believe in the company's values, and introduces the concept of the Golden Circle Model to elucidate how exemplary leaders motivate actions when developing great companies—the model revolves around a purpose, cause, or belief—the "Why." Contrary to the conventional sequence of addressing "What," "How," and then "Why," Sinek argues that inspired leaders and organizations invert this order to "Why," "How," and then "What." This approach underlines the idea that people are drawn not to the specifics of what you do, but to the reasons behind your actions.

Furthermore, Sinek draws parallels between the Golden Circle Model[*] and the structure of the human brain. He points out that the neocortex, which is responsible for rational thoughts, aligns with the "What" aspect, while the limbic system, which governs emotions and behaviors, corresponds to the "How" and "Why." This alignment suggests that starting communications with "What" fails to engage emotions or drive behavior. By contrast, beginning with "Why" and progressing to "What" effectively taps into emotional responses and behaviors.

Now, let's contemplate the elements that define organizational culture for a great company. To me, the *culture of great organizations has the specific role of revolving around the mission and values that empower and stimulate employee creativity within the framework of a clear structure.*

Let's explore an example, which is quite well known.

In 2002, Google was still a relatively small company and Larry Page, the CEO, was working on the project "AdWords engine," which was not working as intended—it would indeed seem a basic task to match search terms to appropriate ads. Larry pinned a note to Google's kitchen wall, with examples of these failures and his own verdict about them: "THESE ADS SUCK"; then he left. It was Friday afternoon. The next Monday, early in the morning, Larry received an email with a proposed fix. Apparently, some Googlers had voluntarily worked over the weekend to find a successful solution. The team had worked on it without asking

---

[*] In *Start with Why*, Simon Sinek discusses how Apple Inc. embraces the Golden Circle model in various sections of the book. He explains that Apple's success can be attributed to its ability to start with "why"—its core belief and purpose—which attracts consumers who share similar beliefs. This approach, according to Sinek, contrasts with other companies that start with "what" they do and "how" they do it, which doesn't inspire the same loyalty and enthusiasm from customers.

Specifically, Sinek elaborates on Apple's application of the Golden Circle in their marketing and product development strategies to create a strong, loyal following. He uses Apple as a key example to illustrate how starting with "why" can differentiate a company and make it more successful than others that focus primarily on products or services.

permission. They did not have any responsibility for the ads project. Note that, by 2014, the AdWords engine was producing $160 million per day in revenue.

What are the takeaways here? I would highlight two, again thinking back on the agile equilibrium we discussed previously:

- In great organizations, employees embrace responsibility and take initiative without fear of failure (freedom)—the employees at Google took the initiative on something even if it was not their project;
- In great organizations, employees have a clear understanding of the main business priorities (structure)—the team at Google knew that "AdWords" was a major business priority.

What is interesting is that this is a rule more than an exception at Google; the company actively fosters a culture of taking initiative within a structured framework by developing policies around it. For instance, consider the 80-20 rule that Google pioneered and which other companies have since adopted. This policy allows Google employees to dedicate 80 percent of their time to core projects while spending the remaining 20 percent on projects they are passionate about. According to some literature, several major innovations have emerged from this 20 percent of the time.

A similar culture based on taking initiative while having clear direction can be observed in other great companies. For instance, at Netflix, the ethos is encapsulated in how teams are empowered to take responsibility and action to do what is best for the company. Netflix stands out as a fascinating example of an organization with a remarkable culture.

Let's look at what the Netflix Manifesto[†] says: "In some organizations, there is an unhealthy emphasis on process and not much freedom … Specifically, many organizations have freedom and responsibility when they are small and everyone knows each other. As they grow, however, their business gets more complex and they add a lot of rules."

[†] Netflix Manifesto. https://jobs.netflix.com/culture.

From these quote, it seems clear that the company tries to avoid an unhealthy obsession with processes, especially as the organization grows.

However, while championing freedom, a closer examination of Netflix culture reveals a well-defined structure within the company, with clear roles and responsibilities, protocols, communication channels, and so on. By no means does this imply an absence of rules; instead, it underscores the significance of clear direction and protocols, and essential practices for decision making, running meetings and so on.

So, while the culture champions freedom, it equally underscores responsibility and accountability.

Aligning Vision With Purpose

The cornerstone of a company's culture is a clear vision and mission, which fosters a collective belief among employees and defines why a company exists.

What's lacking in many organizations, particularly traditional ones, is as follows:

- A clear mission and vision that permeate the company's values and culture;
- Employees who genuinely believe in it and live by their values.[‡]

The clarity of the mission and vision is crucial,[§] as it influences the company's culture and the alignment of individual and organizational purposes. Let's take the case of Joy de Vivre' Hotels,[5] an amazing company I researched whose mission is to create joy for its employees

---

[‡] Sometimes, I tell my students the example of Enron. Enron is an example of a company that espoused high values such as integrity and excellence, but whose employees did not genuinely believe in or practice these values. Despite their stated commitment to ethical standards, the company was ultimately exposed for massive fraud, highlighting the discrepancy between their proclaimed values and actual practices.

[§] Let's clarify that this book does not delve deeply into analyzing the vision/mission of great companies, including their intense focus on the customer, as it is beyond its intended scope. What I wanted to highlight here is how employees need to believe in and understand what the mission and vision of the company is.

and customers. In this company, the engagement of employees revolves around alignment and contribution.

To give one example, at one of their boutique hotels, the management team launched an initiative allowing staff to design personalized guest experiences based on the guest's reason for visiting—this was part of the main mission of the company to improve customer experience. Whether it was creating a bespoke itinerary for a couple celebrating an anniversary or arranging a unique city tour for history buffs, employees were encouraged to use their insights and creativity to enhance guest stays. This initiative not only increased guest satisfaction but also boosted staff morale and productivity, as employees felt directly connected to the hotel's mission and empowered to make a meaningful impact. *When employees understand how their individual and collective efforts contribute to the company's mission, it serves as a powerful motivator, ultimately leading to higher productivity* (we will discuss this later while discussing objectives and key results [OKRs]).

As former CEO of LinkedIn Jeff Weiner put it, "the most successful companies at scale are the ones where the employees talk about the challenges, we, face versus what, the company, faces. If there is a big challenge, it's easy to blame it on their external, the company, but the truth is—they are the company. The leadership is the people who run the company—and this is not just the executives but everyone in the company."[6] ⸷

This aligns with the concept Simon Sinek emphasized—knowing your "why" goes beyond just "what" you do. ** Understanding the deeper purpose, especially in relation to the broader mission, contributes significantly to organizational culture and employee motivation.

⸷ The article discusses Jeff Weiner's lecture at Stanford University, where he addressed scaling LinkedIn. The session delved into how the right company culture and strategic planning are essential for effectively managing growth at scale. It highlighted how LinkedIn developed a culture that supports scaling, emphasizing the importance of alignment, execution, and adaptation in rapidly growing organizations.

** In *Start with Why*, Simon Sinek emphasizes that knowing your "why" goes beyond just "what" you do.

Innovative Hiring Practices

What I find interesting is that great companies always highlight the idea that recruiting is one of the most important things a company does. This makes sense, doesn't it? At the end of the day, what is a company if not the employees that work in it?

Now, this *balance between freedom and structure also permeates the hiring process in many of those great organizations.*

Indeed, great companies often have innovative protocols in place to hire people and they also continue to experiment and test new ways of doing so.

For instance, I was fascinated when I read about a company called "Menlo Innovations" in San Francisco and their innovative hiring process.[7] The company management thought that traditional recruitment methods didn't always yield optimal results, as they initially relied on resumes and interviews, which could leave uncertainty about whether a candidate is truly the right fit for the team or the company. Not only that, what the company realized is that many individuals realize that the work or the organization is not aligned with their expectations only after joining it.

I have observed that myself. As a recruiter in some organizations, it was difficult for me to understand whether a candidate would be fit for the proposed role based on the techniques we used to select him or her. As a potential candidate, I often also found it difficult to understand whether I was fit for working in a specific organization or team, or not.

So, what is it that Menlo did to bring about some innovation around recruitment?

Menlo developed specific criteria on the type of candidates they looked for, as follows: people who are curious, fast learners, emphasizing adaptability to their unique culture and collaborative work approach.

Second, they developed a specific process that includes the following steps:

1. The company crafts an engaging job announcement and invites 30-50 potential candidates based on specific criteria. They send materials and videos to these candidates.

2. The company's mission and vision is presented to the participants.

3. Then, the company conducts three 20-minute simulations. Each
   candidate collaborates with another candidate for 20 minutes in
   various exercises, such as estimating project development time,
   incorporating elements into a project within a given budget,
   and other visual exercises. All activities are conducted without
   the use of computers. The goal is to test collaboration rather
   than technical skills. Observers from the company (one observer
   for every two candidates) assess the collaboration, pondering
   questions such as "Would I like to work with this person? Will
   they be helpful? Will I learn from them?" This is followed by a
   brief Q&A session and an opportunity to draft a follow-up email
   for feedback (with the reward of choosing a book, to be sent to
   their homes).

4. Observers convene to discuss their observations, spending five
   minutes on each candidate. The key question is whether they
   would want to work with the candidate. Observers vote with
   a thumbs up or thumbs down. If all observers give a thumbs
   up, there is no further discussion, and the candidate proceeds to
   the next stage. In case of a thumbs down or lack of consensus,
   there is a discussion on whether the candidate aligns with the
   company culture. The CEO may intervene, but if they were not
   an observer, they cannot vote. Selected candidates are invited to
   the second round.

5. Then they invite the selected candidates for a day of work on
   a concrete project. The morning session involves working with
   one team member. Then the afternoon session is with another
   team member. The objective is to assess the candidate's technical
   proficiency and, equally importantly, to help them understand
   the company's work environment. Candidates are encouraged
   to ask questions and actively participate. After the day, they
   are compensated for their time. The two team members the
   candidate worked with, along with the along with the planning

manager (who also handles HR-related responsibilities), convene to provide feedback.

6. If the feedback is positive, the selected individual is offered a three-week trial employment contract.

The Ideal Candidate: Traits of Top Performers

We have just mentioned quickly some of the characteristics Menlo looks for in prospective candidates. What is interesting, however, is that great companies look for somewhat similar skills when they are hiring people. They do so no matter what sector the company operates in.

Some of the most coveted skills I would like to highlight are the following:

- Leadership and listening
- Creativity
- Team orientation
- Cognitive ability
- Self-discipline
- Bias for action
- Fast learners
- Independent thinking

Among some of the main skills of prospective candidates, *great companies seem to look for people who discipline themselves (structure) and, at the same time, who take initiative (freedom).*

Let's take as an example Semco, a company that is involved in a variety of business sectors, including manufacturing, environmental services, and real estate. Semco adopts a distinctive approach to removing traditional corporate hierarchies by focusing on hiring individuals who are self-disciplined and proactive—in other words, people who are capable of managing themselves. The company implicitly aims to treat its employees as "responsible adults," a stark contrast to many traditional work environments where employees are micromanaged like adolescents. Outside of work, these individuals make significant life decisions, contribute to their communities, and lead their families. Yet, in many companies, they face restrictive rules that require them to wear badges, adhere to strict schedules, and ask permission for basic needs. Semco respects and utilizes their mature capabilities, allowing employees to bring their full adult selves to their roles, and thus fostering a more responsible and engaged workforce.[8]

Through both my readings and personal reflections, I've discovered that great companies cultivate environments where employees are not just empowered but also encouraged to take initiative.

Yet, taking the Agile Equilibrium Framework into account, the employees do take initiative but they do so while knowing what the direction, main priorities, and protocols of the company are.

Indeed, great companies do train employees on the company's protocols and practices so that they are aware of them. I read about an interesting organization called "Buurtzorg," which is made up of teams of around 10,000 nurses.[9] Now, in this company, new team members undergo training in problem-solving, meeting practices, and even self-management—again trying to find a balance between empowering employees to take initiatives while giving them some structure at the same time.

One skill great companies also prioritize, which I find particularly interesting, especially given the discussion about organizational fear we mentioned earlier in traditional companies, is related to "independent thinking." I remember reading about Bridgewater Associates, one of the world's largest hedge funds, where founder Ray Dalio emphasizes hiring individuals capable of critical thinking and challenging prevailing perspectives.

Dalio believes that innovation comes from diversity of thought, which is why he actively seeks out candidates who demonstrate the ability to think independently. This means hiring individuals who are not afraid to question the status quo, propose novel ideas, and engage in constructive debates. Bridgewater's culture is built on the principle of radical transparency (we will discuss this later), where every employee is encouraged to voice their opinions and challenge assumptions, regardless of their position within the company. This environment fosters a dynamic where diverse viewpoints are not only welcomed but are also seen as essential to the organization's success.

By empowering employees to think critically and independently, Bridgewater aims to mitigate groupthink and avoid the pitfalls of conventional wisdom. This approach ensures that decisions are made based on a comprehensive analysis of various perspectives, leading to more robust and innovative solutions. Furthermore, it cultivates a culture of continuous learning and improvement, where employees are motivated to constantly seek out new knowledge and challenge their own thinking.

In this way, great companies such as Bridgewater Associates recognize that fostering independent thinking among their employees is crucial for driving innovation and maintaining a competitive edge. By empowering individuals to think critically and challenge prevailing perspectives, these organizations create an environment where creativity and innovation can thrive.

Reimagining Organizational Structures While Focusing on People

Navigating the delicate equilibrium between structure and freedom prompts *great companies to re-evaluate traditional management structures, including the use of organizational charts.*

Remarkably, some companies have entirely dispensed with traditional organizational charts, job descriptions, and titles. What they do is to emphasize roles and responsibilities that evolve based on the needs of the organization and the talents of individuals rather than mere titles and positions. This approach challenges the conventional wisdom of fitting individuals into predefined job roles.

Take, for example, FAVI, a leading brass foundry that has rejected the traditional organizational chart.[10] FAVI operates on a model where the factory is segmented into autonomous "mini-plants," each responsible for its own costs and judged by its own results. This structure promotes accountability and flexibility, diverging from standard corporate practices. Instead of a hierarchical management structure, in

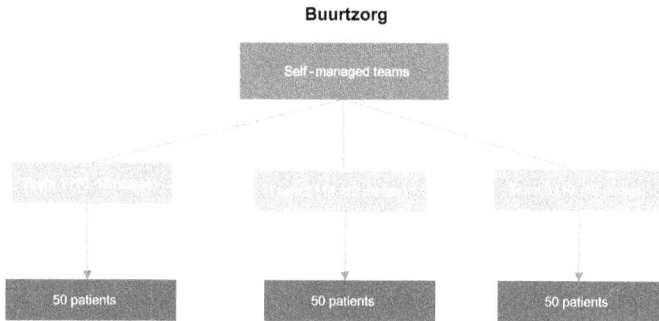

Figure 4.2 Organizational self-management structure at Buurtzorg
Source: Developed by the author

each mini-plant, FAVI employs a team leader who oversees management roles, thereby fostering a more collaborative and agile environment.

Similarly, companies such as Zappos have experimented with holacracy, a decentralized management system where roles are defined by the team members themselves, allowing for self-organization and greater adaptability. This model illustrates a shift toward empowering employees to shape their work environment, reflecting a balance between structured roles and the freedom to innovate within those roles.[11]

Another interesting company we already mentioned, Buurtzorg, adopts the principles of self-management, without establishing a traditional hierarchy. In this company, for instance, *the teams of nurses plan their patient visits, vacation schedules, and other logistics autonomously, distributing tasks among themselves without a designated boss.* The nurses organize themselves into teams of 10 to 12, each responsible for a group of 50 patients, as shown in Figure 4.2.

The fascinating part of the story is that they make decisions collectively, without a hierarchical structure. In many traditional organizations, management typically handles tasks like budget estimates, often relying on limited information. In innovative organizations like Buurtzorg, those directly involved in the work—the nurses—make the decisions. Isn't it a more logical approach—to decentralize decision making and empower employees?

It is important to note that the underlying principle here is *not the outright rejection of organizational charts, but instead a focus on people, their interactions, and how they can best work together without being constrained by rigid titles and job descriptions.*

This ethos is echoed by Ricardo Semler, former CEO of Semco—who we mentioned earlier—who criticized traditional hierarchical structures for stifling productivity and creativity. Semco introduced an "organizational circle," significantly flattening the hierarchy to just three levels and redefining leadership roles to encourage closer alignment between planning and execution. This model represents a radical departure from conventional corporate pyramids, aiming to enhance communication and collaboration across the organization.[12]

Menlo Innovations, which we previously mentioned, also offers a compelling case study. While maintaining job titles and a form of organizational chart, Menlo emphasizes role fluidity, allowing employees to explore different roles based on their interests and the needs of the company. This practice underscores the importance of focusing on individuals' skills and their potential to contribute in various capacities, aligning with the concept of a portfolio career and the value of a broad range of experiences.

Other great companies have also experimented with their organizational structure. At one extreme, the music-streaming service Spotify has fundamentally changed its organizational structure.[13] The company's product-delivery organization is made up of squads, tribes, chapters, and guilds. The primary unit is the squad, a multidisciplinary team that works toward a shared purpose and is run by a product owner. Tribes are groups of squads that work on related areas. Chapters are groups of people with similar expertise across squads. Guilds are interest groups that anyone can join. Other companies have simply overlaid cross-functional teams above the existing hierarchy.

The practices developed by those companies illustrate the fact that finding a balance between structure and freedom involves reimagining traditional organizational models. By prioritizing people over rigid structures, fostering flexibility, and encouraging a culture of collaboration, organizations can create environments where innovation and creativity flourish.

Ensuring Order Without Chaos Can Lead to Higher Productivity

While experimenting with traditional organizational practices, the companies I just mentioned have all achieved outstanding results in the past—all these companies have been quite high-performing. For instance, Buurtzorg, which, as I said, has experimented with self-management practices, has grown into a network of 10,000 nurses achieved outstanding levels of care, according to studies and research, including the 2009 E&Y.[14]

Similarly, under the leadership of Ricardo Semler, Semco has experienced significant growth. Reports from various sources, including Semler's own writings, have indicated that Semco's revenue grew from $4 million in the 1980s to over $212 million in the early 2000s.[††]

Detailed financial results for Menlo Innovations are not publicly disclosed, like many privately held companies. However, the success of Menlo Innovations can be inferred from several indirect indicators such as its sustained business and growth; the company has been in operation since 2001, indicating its ability to sustain and grow its business over time. The company has also had the ability to attract and retain a diverse range of projects and clients, including both start-ups and large corporations, which is another indicator of its financial health. And finally, the company has received awards and recognition from many industry groups, business associations, and the media.

Another company we can mention here that has experimented with its organizational structure while maintaining a high profitability is W. L. Gore & Associates. The company, which is globally renowned for its innovative products and unique organizational structure, operates without a traditional hierarchical management structure and is famous for its flat organization where all employees are referred to as "associates" and are encouraged to communicate directly with one another. This flat structure eliminates formal chains of command, promoting high levels of collaboration and innovation. Associates are encouraged to follow their commitments rather than orders from a superior, which cultivates an environment of trust and mutual respect. This approach

---

[††] https://en.wikipedia.org/wiki/Ricardo_Semler.

not only empowers employees but also aligns closely with the company's core philosophy of personal initiative and creativity within a supportive framework. Gore's model demonstrates how removing traditional hierarchies can lead to enhanced productivity and innovation, as seen in their diverse product lines, from GORE-TEX fabric to medical devices, all stemming from the associates' freedom to explore new ideas and take ownership of their projects.

This company is indeed recognized as one of the world's best multinational workplaces by great place to work.[15] But what about its profitability? According to Forbes, the company generates annual revenues of $4.8 billion.[16]

Exploring how organizations like these—among numerous others—succeed without a traditional hierarchical system reveals a compelling story. These entities demonstrate a profound sense of structure, not derived from an overabundance of the rules and guidelines characteristic of conventional organizations, but from a strong, clear mission and vision, coupled with fundamental principles that empower employees to take initiative. This could be described as a sort of structured or disciplined freedom.

Simplifying Complexity and Reducing Procedures for Greater Efficiency

This approach to organizational design, which some great companies have experimented, is essentially an exercise in simplification. Those companies cut through the clutter of unnecessary steps and rules, focusing instead on streamlining processes.

Ricardo Semler of Semco, for instance, eliminated excessive norms and regulations, advocating for a reliance on common sense over rigid, often counterproductive rules. This philosophy underscores a preference for personal accountability over bureaucracy.

This sentiment also echoes through the so-called "Friction Project," and its corresponding publication, which critiques the human propensity to accumulate rather than streamline—a tendency that can stifle productivity and innovation. Authored by Bob Sutton and Huggy Rao[17] and featured in the *Harvard Business Review*, this initiative highlights the importance of maintaining only those rules and protocols that genuinely enhance work efficiency and ensure safety.

Again, the main point here isn't to discard structure (as the CEO of Menlo Innovation puts it, "If a structured process is useful and easy to understand and use, there's no reason not to adopt it"[18]) entirely, but to refine and simplify it, stripping away superfluous procedures while preserving those that are genuinely beneficial.

This balance is crucial, allowing for both responsibility and creativity within a structured framework.

The book *Joy, Inc.*, which describes the culture and practices of Menlo, offers further insight into this philosophy, particularly in a chapter called "End Chaos, Eliminate Ambiguity."[19] Indeed, the company employs protocols that are both practical and straightforward, reinforcing the notion that useful and understandable systems should be readily adopted, an approach far removed from chaos, and embodying structured or disciplined freedom.

When I was reading about NASA,[20] I realized that, even for this company, the same principle holds true. Following the Challenger disaster, NASA tried to define bedrock principles that must be followed to avoid chaos, and distinguish them from the areas where rigid adherence to detailed rules is counterproductive. For instance, in designing the International Space Station, some elements needed to be clearly defined—for instance, the hardware that connects different parts of the station that were built by different countries. Beyond that, the station design allowed for variations that enabled agencies to use techniques that have been developed and valued over time.

Employees should have clarity over dimensions such as the mission and main protocols to follow, but also room to take initiatives.

Empowering Employees Within a Structured Framework

As we said earlier in our discussion, the empowerment of employees is a significant driver of motivation, which, in turn, boosts productivity (freedom and autonomy). We also quickly mentioned that for autonomy to be effective, it must be coupled with purpose.

Employees not only need to align with the company's mission but also to understand and see their individual contributions as part of the company's larger objectives. This sense of alignment is essential. Let us now discuss this important subject in detail.

One practical tool for achieving company's alignment is the OKR methodology. This strategy is used by high-profile organizations such as LinkedIn, Twitter, Oracle, Dropbox, and Coursera among others. The power of OKRs lies in their ability to establish cascading objectives, connecting overarching company goals with the specific objectives of departments and teams. This not only clarifies expectations but also harmonizes individual efforts with the company's strategic ambitions.

John Doerr famously explained how OKRs were implemented in a sports organization about American Football to illustrate its impact.[21] In the example (Figure 4.3), the general manager's objective is "Make money for the owner" with two key results: (1). "Win the Super Bowl" and (2). "Fill the stands to at least 90 percent capacity." Here's how the OKRs cascade down the team:

1. General Manager: Cascades his goal to the head coach and the Senior Vice President of marketing. His key results become their objectives.

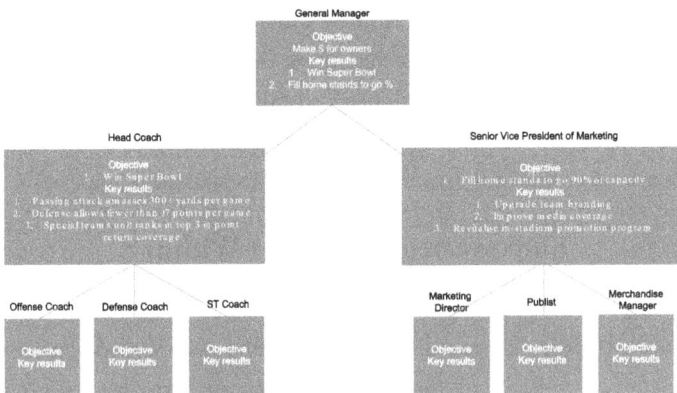

Figure 4.3 OKRs—alignment and contribution

Source: Adapted from Doerr, J. Measure *What Matters: How Google, Bono, and the Gates Foundation Rock the World with OKRs*

2. Head Coach: Develops three key results and cascades them to the offense coach, defense coach, and special teams coach, who then devise their own key results.

3. Senior Vice President of Marketing: Derives his objective from the general manager's key result, "Fill the stands to 90 percent capacity," and crafts three key results. These become the objectives for the marketing director, publicist, and merchandise manager, who do not devise their own key results but follow the SVP's directives.

OKRs should be transparent across the organization and not always cascade through hierarchical layers. Objectives can jump levels, for example, from a CEO directly to a manager. An optimal OKR system balances alignment with autonomy, allowing contributors to set some of their own OKRs. When individuals set their own OKRs, they are more likely to stretch beyond expectations and achieve ambitious targets.

This approach is indeed deeply intertwined with the organization's culture, particularly concerning the essential elements of transparency and communication, which we've previously mentioned, ensuring that all employees are informed, engaged, and aligned with the company's strategic objectives.

Transparency and Communication as Foundations of Great Companies

Transparency and communication are fundamental elements for companies to achieve greatness, as visualized in the Agile Equilibrium Framework. These cross-cutting principles underpin many successful organizational practices.

Let's take the OKR approach again. The visibility of everyone's OKRs within the company is crucial. Google exemplifies this practice by incorporating OKRs into its staff biographies, ensuring that each employee's goals and objectives are openly accessible to all. This openness not only fosters a culture of accountability but also encourages a shared sense of purpose and direction across the organization.

Transparency and communication stand as cornerstone practices within all the great companies I've encountered.

For instance, the "Work Authorization Board" at Menlo, featured in *Joy, Inc.,* is a testament to this; the ongoing projects and the assigned team members are clearly displayed and frequently updated for the whole company.[22] The board is laid out as a rectangular matrix with story cards pinned to the wall, organized by the day of the week and the pair of individuals collaborating on each project.

This notion of openness also extends to financial information. Many forward-thinking organizations opt to share comprehensive financial data with their employees, although there are a few exceptions. Upon reflection, however, the logic is clear; teams tasked with decision making and responsibility must be equipped with all pertinent information to make informed choices. At Google there are routine all-hands meetings where quarterly results are shared, and this has become a standard practice. Similarly, LinkedIn CEO Jeff Weiner would conduct weekly all-hands meetings to discuss company priorities and challenges, maintaining a dialogue that spanned globally across many cities around the world.[23] These sessions were crucial for reiterating priorities, celebrating successes, and addressing areas of concern in an open manner.

At Semco, the company operates on three interdependent core values: democracy or employee involvement, profit sharing, and information. The synergy of these values is critical; the absence of one would render the others ineffective. This ethos of communication translates into empowering employees with transparency. Semco ensures that all team members are educated on how to interpret financial documents—training provided by their union. On a monthly basis, each employee receives key financial documents for their division, fostering a sense of ownership and insight. But simplification also plays a key role; Semco utilizes a streamlined accounting system that offers clear and actionable data, enabling quick and informed decision making. This approach is not unique to Semco, but is part of a broader trend among innovative companies that trust their employees.

Trusting Employees to Make Organizations More Human

Trust is a foundational element in these organizational models. As discussed earlier, companies that integrate transparency and open communication foster a culture of trust by openly sharing information with their employees. This transparency not only empowers employees but also significantly enhances organizational dynamics and employee engagement.

These companies place a high level of trust in their employees, believing in their inherent capability and responsibility. By sharing information openly, they create an environment where employees feel valued and respected, leading to greater motivation and a stronger sense of ownership in their work.

Central to the success of these initiatives are trust and open communication, along with respect and integrity. Great organizations operate on the belief that people are inherently capable and trustworthy.

This is exemplified by the approach of FAVI's former CEO Jean François Zobrist, which, in turn, is reminiscent of Douglas McGregor's Theory Y and Theory W.[‡‡] These theories suggest that, if you view your team members as self-motivated and satisfied in their work, you're more inclined to have a participative management style. Such managers trust their employees to take initiative and manage their tasks independently, as opposed to the controlling and micromanaging nature of Theory X management. For example, FAVI's experience, illustrates this. The removal of factory time clocks led to employees staying longer than

---

[‡‡] McGregor's Theory X and Theory Y are two contrasting sets of assumptions about the nature of people at work.

Theory X posits that employees are inherently lazy, dislike work, and will avoid it if they can. It assumes that workers need to be closely supervised and controlled with strict rules and punishments, as they lack self-motivation and require external direction to achieve organizational goals.

Theory Y, on the other hand, suggests that employees are self-motivated, enjoy their job duties, and work to better themselves without direct incentive. This theory assumes that workers can be self-directed and creative if given a conducive work environment. Managers who adhere to Theory Y believe that under the right conditions, employees will seek out responsibility and that the satisfaction of doing a good job is a strong motivation.

their shift, not because they were clock-watching, but because they felt a sense of responsibility for their work. Zobrist recognized that trusting employees and simplifying procedures not only saved costs but also fostered a more responsible workforce.

Ricardo Semler's practices with Semco in Brazil also exemplify this trust toward employees. Semler would lead a company where the employees, including factory workers, are treated as responsible adults. They set their own hours, are privy to the company's financials, and partake in major company decisions, embodying the spirit of Theory Y.

Granting trust does indeed foster a sense of responsibility within an organization, as employees emulate their peers and take ownership of their work, having been imbued with a belief in its value and purpose.

This concept dovetails with the idea of *humanizing organizations*[24]— *placing people at the heart of corporate culture.* The world's most progressive companies strive to create environments that recognize and embrace the full humanity of their employees. Rather than enforcing rigid codes for dress and office hours, these organizations focus on individual needs and allow for personal expression.

For example, Menlo Innovations has adopted a family-friendly policy that allows parents to bring their babies to work when child care falls through.[25] This practice acknowledges the complex realities of parenting and supports employees during challenging times.

Similarly, the introduction of pets into the workplace and flexible scheduling are other ways that companies demonstrate their commitment to a humane work environment. Such measures can enhance the well-being of employees, leading to a more relaxed, productive atmosphere.

Earlier, we discussed the concept of "wholeness," which resonated well with what we are discussing here—the idea that great organizations encourage their employees to drop the "masks" they might wear in traditional corporate settings. By enabling individuals to be their authentic selves at work, these companies foster an environment where people feel free to express their individuality and creativity, and to contribute their best without restraint.

Debunking Myths: Agile Equilibrium in the Public Sector

We have been discussing how great companies have adopted principles of the agile equilibrium, striking a balance between freedom and structure. Now, let's explore the extent to which these principles are being applied within the public sector, which is often perceived as excessively bureaucratic.

Reflecting on my experiences working with international organizations and governments worldwide, it's clear that the public sector operates under unique constraints that can make innovation more challenging and performance less dynamic than in the private sector. The public sector is often seen as hierarchical, rule-bound, risk-averse, and somewhat stifling when it comes to employee empowerment and innovation. However, it's important to recognize that the public sector has demonstrated significant capacity for innovation, from the inception of the internet by Defense Advanced Research Projects Agency (DARPA) to the establishment of current innovation labs within government entities.

There are increasingly interesting examples of public sector innovation. For instance, two governments have recently become synonymous with public sector innovation, each launching impactful initiatives that showcase their commitment to agility and modernization:

- Estonia: Known for its digital governance, Estonia introduced the e-Residency program, which allows global citizens to start and manage businesses in Estonia online from anywhere in the world. This initiative is part of a broader digital transformation in the country that includes digital voting, e-health records, and online tax systems, making government services more accessible and efficient. Estonia's agility is exemplified by its ability to rapidly implement and scale digital solutions across the public sector. The development and deployment of its e-Residency program showcased agile methodologies, allowing the government to iteratively improve the platform based on user feedback from a global audience.

- Singapore: The Smart Nation initiative embodies the country's approach to innovation in the public sector. Projects under this initiative include the development of a national digital identity system that simplifies residents' access to public services and enhances the security of online transactions. Additionally, Singapore has been a pioneer in integrating artificial intelligence (AI) in health care, deploying AI-driven systems to predict patient admissions and optimize bed management across hospitals. Singapore's agility is evident in its Smart Nation initiative, particularly through its proactive approach to integrating technology like AI in public services. The national digital identity system was rapidly developed and deployed, illustrating an agile process that involved iterative testing and feedback loops with citizens to ensure effectiveness and ease of use.

I would like to provide two concrete examples of how public sector initiatives are applying some of the principles of agile equilibrium. One example focuses on agile procurement, and the other on the portfolio approach.

Agile procurement: The European Commission (EC) faced the challenge of outsourcing their Information Technology (IT) functions to enhance efficiency and adaptability. Traditionally, this would involve a rigid, lengthy process focused on detailed specifications and fixed contracts, which often led to delays and inflexibility. To address these issues, the EC adopted an agile procurement approach. Initially, they conducted thorough market research and engaged with potential suppliers through consultations. This early engagement helped understand the latest trends and capabilities in IT services. Instead of setting fixed, detailed requirements upfront, the EC defined high-level objectives that allowed for flexibility and adaptation as the project progressed. To streamline the procurement process, long-term framework contracts were established spanning six years with multiple IT consulting firms. These contracts allowed for decentralized purchasing, empowering individual departments to select the most suitable suppliers for specific tasks. During the execution phase, the project was managed in iterative sprints. Each sprint involved close collaboration between the institutions and the suppliers, focusing on delivering minimum viable products (MVPs) that could be tested and improved upon. This iterative process enabled quick adjustments based on feedback and changing needs, ensuring that the final solution was highly effective and up-to-date with the latest technological advancements. Throughout the project, there were no rigid walls between the suppliers and the institutions. Instead, suppliers actively participated in project management, contributing their expertise to ensure success. Pricing was handled progressively, with budgets allocated for each sprint and prices negotiated based on the evolving scope of work. This agile approach significantly reduced administrative burdens and enhanced the project's responsiveness to changes. It allowed the European institutions to maintain productivity, ensure high-quality deliverables, and effectively manage costs.

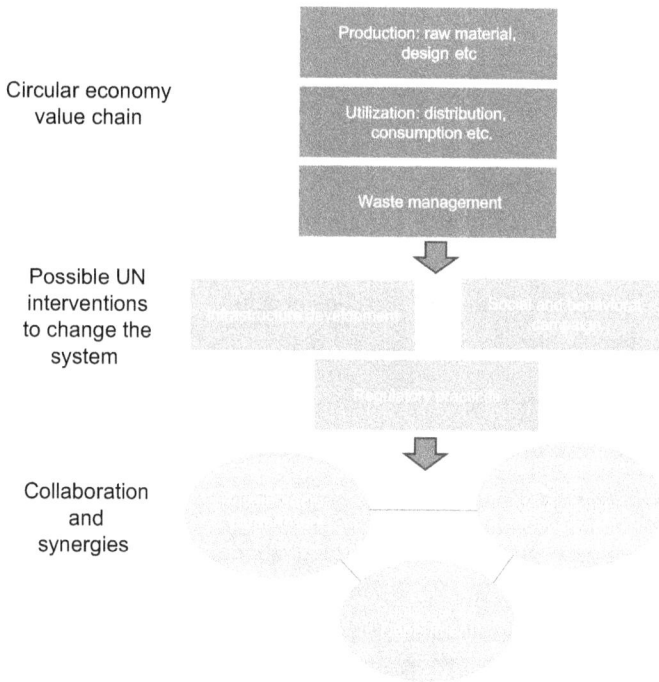

Figure 4.4 Portfolio approach—innovation in public sector

Source: Developed by the author

Portfolio approach: In my involvement with the United Nations, we adopted an innovative methodology known as the "portfolio approach" (Figure 4.4). This strategy was developed to comprehensively design, test, learn from, and scale a variety of interventions that collectively aim to transform complex systems by engaging at multiple levels simultaneously. This approach emerged from the understanding that a single intervention would be insufficient for sustainable change.

Adopting the portfolio approach required a significant shift from the UN's traditional operations. It necessitated enhanced cross-departmental collaboration and communication, moving away from the siloed structures. Let me illustrate this with our circular economy program in an Asian country.

We began by mapping the ecosystem, identifying all stakeholders involved in the circular economy. This included government agencies, private companies, nongovernmental organizations (NGOs), and local communities. We then developed a value chain for the circular economy, highlighting problematic areas and pain points that hindered sustainable practices.

Within the waste management segment of the value chain, for instance, several key issues were identified:

1. Lack of Infrastructure: Insufficient recycling facilities and waste-processing plants.
2. Limited Public Awareness: Low levels of community engagement and understanding of recycling benefits.
3. Regulatory Gaps: Inadequate policies and enforcement mechanisms.

To address these problems, we developed interventions targeting different parts of the system:

1. Infrastructure Development: Collaborating with the private sector, we initiated projects to build new recycling facilities and upgrade existing ones. This involved public–private partnerships where the government provided incentives and the private sector brought in technology and investment.

2. Public Awareness Campaigns: We worked with NGOs and local community leaders to launch educational campaigns. These campaigns aimed to raise awareness about the benefits of recycling and encourage community participation in waste management efforts.

3. Regulatory Reforms: The public sector played a crucial role in revising and enforcing waste management policies. This included setting up stricter regulations for waste disposal, incentivizing recycling, and penalizing noncompliance.

The success of these interventions would therefore rely heavily on the synergy between different sectors. The public sector would need to provide the regulatory framework and infrastructure investment. The private sector would need to bring innovation and funding and help on the infrastructure development, while social development organizations would need to engage communities and ensured grassroots participation.

The Scalability Paradox

One challenge that is unique to both public sector organizations and large corporations is the sheer size of the organization. It is natural to question whether their extensive scale constrains their ability to maintain agility and innovative practices.

The relationship between an organization's size and its performance is indeed a nuanced one.

My research has shown that size does not always preclude greatness. For example, the global energy provider Applied Energy Services (AES), with more than 40,000 employees, has adopted innovative practices and experimented with self-managed teams, each with the autonomy to manage their investment budgets. Buurtzorg, with its team of 10,000 nurses, also challenges the notion that larger organizations lack agility.

However, when a company scales up, it can lead to either too much structure or too much freedom, creating issues.

Spotify is an interesting example of a company that encountered some issues when they grow too fast and expand their personnel by developing "too much structure" leading to inefficiency. The CEO of Spotify recently addressed the challenges of growing and scaling up in a companywide email, acknowledging the need for adjustments: "When we look back on 2022 and 2023, it has truly been impressive what we have accomplished. But, at the same time, the reality is much of this output was linked to having more resources. ... Today, we still have too many people dedicated to supporting work and even doing work around the work rather than contributing to opportunities with real impact. More people need to be focused on delivering for our key stakeholders—creators and consumers. In two words, we have to become relentlessly resourceful."[26]

It is also essential to recognize that, while some great companies struggle when scaling up and getting too much "structure," such as in the example of Spotify, the opposite is true of companies getting too much freedom. When companies are given excessive freedom without adequate guidance, it can lead to confusion and inefficiency, undermining their potential for growth and success. The more freedom we give, the more clarity about mission, vision, strategy, and values is required to maintain focus and direction.

For instance, Outcon, a tech start-up known for its lax operational guidelines and innovative practices, initially benefited from a high degree of freedom, encouraging innovation and rapid development. However, as the company grew, this lack of structure led to misaligned objectives and project delays, highlighting the need for a balanced approach.[27] Similarly, companies that champion radical autonomy must also invest heavily in clear and consistent communication of their mission and values to prevent disarray and ensure that all team members are aligned toward common goals.

So, what is required as organizations grow larger to continue innovating and working effectively?

Balancing Scalability and Innovation

A common pattern I have observed in many great companies is their tendency to divide into smaller, more manageable units and teams, even as they grow in size, to maintain a balance between structure and flexibility .

At Semco, a decision to keep units small led to the division of a facility that had grown over 300 employees suggesting that there's a limit to the number of small teams that can function effectively within a large entity. Alphabet Inc. adopted a similar strategy, restructuring into a collection of smaller companies under one umbrella. Within each of those companies, smaller teams are created to work effectively.

This echoes the writer Antony Jay who noted[28] that, historically, humans are accustomed to working in small groups. He also noted that the advent of the Industrial Revolution thrust workers into massive factories, creating a disconnect between individual involvement and the organizational structure.

In essence, while size does present challenges, it doesn't automatically hinder an organization's capacity for greatness. The key is to continually adapt, innovate, and perhaps most importantly, ensure that the essence of the company—its culture, values, and principles—remains intact and active, regardless of scale.

It is also important to highlight that, according to research, not every part of an organization needs to adopt agility and become more dynamic. I remember reading an interesting article,[29] "Agile at Scale," suggesting that while agility can be beneficial, it's not universally applicable across all departments. Agile methodologies might not fit every department or function within an organization. Areas with highly regulated processes, for instance, may find it difficult to adopt agile practices fully, due to compliance requirements. Similarly, departments that are not directly involved in product development, such as human resources or finance, may need to adapt agile principles differently in order to make them relevant to their work.

This brings me to the concept of exploration and exploitation. In a way, the concepts of exploration and exploitation are crucial in understanding how organizations can strike a balance between freedom and structure to foster innovation while maintaining operational excellence. These principles, rooted in organizational strategy and innovation management, highlight the importance of simultaneously pursuing new opportunities (exploration) and optimizing current strengths (exploitation). Airbnb exemplifies this by continually innovating, as it did with the introduction of "Experiences" and "Airbnb Plus" for its users. These initiatives—"Experiences," which offers unique cultural engagements, and "Airbnb Plus," which provides premium accommodation—demonstrate how Airbnb is diversifying its services and creating new revenue streams. Crucially, Airbnb has developed these services without straying from its core business model of home-sharing. This strategic expansion shows Airbnb's commitment to innovation and experimentation, seamlessly integrating new offerings that enhance user experience while reinforcing their foundational marketplace.

Exploration embodies the essence of freedom within an organization. It is the pursuit of innovation, venturing into uncharted territories, and embracing risk-taking and experimentation. Exploration is about allowing the creative and innovative spirit to flourish, encouraging individuals and teams to seek out new knowledge, technologies, and processes. This freedom to explore is vital for discovering groundbreaking ideas and solutions that can lead to transformative changes and long-term growth. However, to harness this effectively, organizations need to provide a supportive structure that guides exploratory efforts without stifling creativity.

By contrast, exploitation represents the structured side of the equation. It focuses on leveraging existing resources, knowledge, and capabilities, to achieve efficiency and incremental improvements. Exploitation involves a disciplined approach to refining and enhancing current operations, products, and services, aiming for immediate and tangible outcomes. While this requires a certain level of control and standardization, providing some degree of autonomy within this framework can lead to more engaged and motivated teams, driving better performance and innovation even in the pursuit of exploitation.

Balancing exploration and exploitation is about finding the optimal mix of freedom and structure that allows an organization to innovate and adapt while also capitalizing on its established strengths. This balance, often referred to as organizational ambidexterity, is key to sustaining competitiveness and achieving long-term success.

What we're highlighting here is the possibility within organizations for teams working on both exploration and exploitation, each with their unique strengths and focuses, to operate concurrently. Some teams may thrive on exploration, seeking out new knowledge and innovation, while others excel at exploitation, optimizing and refining existing processes and capabilities.

The journey for a company to become more nimble and agile is complex, as each company needs to navigate the balance between freedom and structure. To add to the complexity, it is also essential to consider the importance of context.

Context Matters

The transformation process to make a company more nimble and more innovative ("great") varies significantly across organizations as it also depends on their existing structures, cultures, practices, and specific contexts. Essentially, every organization is a unique system, so a one-size-fits-all blueprint for innovation doesn't exist.

For instance, while the core principles of creating great organizations can transcend borders, the application of these principles must be sensitively adapted to fit the unique cultural, economic, and social contexts of non-Western countries.

For example, leadership styles that are participatory and less hierarchical may resonate well in cultures that value community and collective decision making. Conversely, in cultures where hierarchical structures are deeply ingrained, sudden shifts to flat organizational structures might face resistance, and could disrupt existing dynamics.

Western principles (such as those around agility) could be effectively applied in non-Western contexts if they find ways to blend globally recognized business practices with local traditions. For instance, a tech start-up in Asia might incorporate global agile management techniques, but may want to adapt their implementation to fit the local work culture, which may value certain hierarchical respects or ritual practices.

In many East Asian cultures, the concept of "face"—a deeply ingrained sense of respect, dignity, and social standing—is essential. Preserving "face" means avoiding embarrassment or shame for oneself and others, fostering a culture of mutual respect and harmony. Companies in these regions often design conflict resolution and feedback mechanisms that respect this principle. For example, instead of providing direct criticism, managers might offer constructive feedback through subtle, indirect communication methods. This ensures that innovation in management practices does not alienate employees or stakeholders by clashing with cultural norms.

As Erin Meyer highlights in *The Culture Map*, understanding cultural nuances, such as the importance of hierarchy and indirect communication in many Asian countries, is critical when integrating global practices like agility. A thoughtful balance between global methodologies and local customs enables organizations to innovate effectively while maintaining cultural sensitivity and employee engagement.

Conclusion

Throughout my exploration of great organizations, whether through literature or firsthand experience, a recurring theme is the balance between freedom and structure—what I term the agile equilibrium. Great companies have indeed applied the principles of this framework and consistently achieved remarkable success. They have embodied this balance by fostering environments where employees are empowered to take initiative and innovate, while maintaining clear missions and strong alignment. This agile equilibrium is the cornerstone of their operational excellence.

What we have seen from this chapter is how these companies have made the principles of the equilibrium operational when it comes to their culture, but also hiring practices, and decision making. Great companies have also experimented on their organizational structures and developed some self-management practices trying to strike a balance between structure and freedom while creating an environment based on communication and trust.

As we have also quickly mentioned, the agile equilibrium and its principles can also be effectively applied when developing high-performing teams (see next).

CHAPTER 5

The Agile Equilibrium at the Team Level

What Constitutes a Performing Team?

A performing team is a group of people who collaborate effectively, allowing enough space for each member to be productive and creative within a structured framework that aligns with the team's purpose and mission.

What it is interesting to note is that *the principles that underpin the success of great companies are just as applicable at the project and team levels.*

My involvement in various projects has shown that adopting management practices that balance freedom and structure within teams is not just beneficial, but necessary. Organizations are, after all, composed of people and teams.

We can therefore refine the focus of the agile equilibrium we have been discussing, from a wide organizational view to a concentrated emphasis on team dynamics (Figure 5.1).

Let us then see how these principles have been applied in team settings. I would like to first provide some personal examples that can shed some light on the main dimensions of high-performing teams in both traditional and start-up organizations. Then we will see how great companies have applied the principles of the framework when it comes to making decision, planning initiatives and budget, and even organizing meetings.

Lessons From Personal Experience: High-Performing Teams in Traditional Organizations

A first example I would like to give is related to my experience in Niger working on the "Rapid Results Initiative" (RRI), which is an action-learning initiative that encourages teams to achieve remarkable results in only 100 days.* This initiative exemplifies how effectively balancing structure and freedom within a project framework can lead to

---

* The Rapid Results Initiative (RRI) is a methodology designed to achieve significant outcomes in a short period, typically within 100 days. It focuses on creating small, dedicated teams tasked with achieving clearly defined and measurable goals. The process empowers teams to innovate and make decisions quickly, fostering a sense of ownership and accountability. This method is often used in contexts where quick, demonstrable progress is needed to build momentum or to overcome bureaucratic inertia.

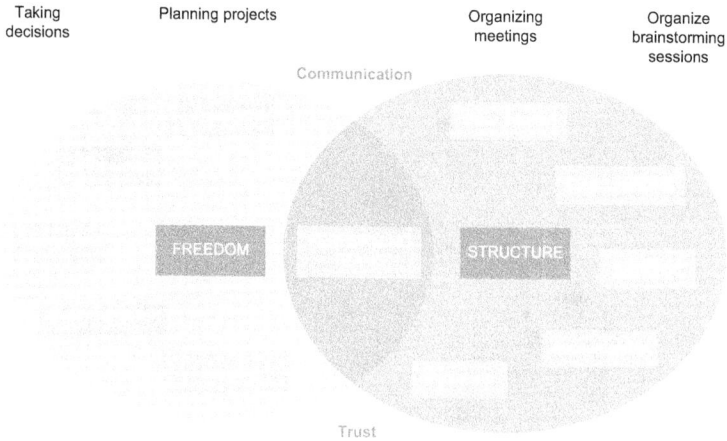

Figure 5.1 High-performing teams

Source: Developed by the author

significant achievements, especially in the challenging context of health care management.

In the early 2010s, while Niger had made some progress on reproductive health and nutrition outcomes, there had been limited movement on some key indicators. For instance, the fertility rate in Niger (about seven births per woman) was among the highest in Sub-Saharan Africa. Additionally, the use of modern contraception for all women had only increased from 12 percent in 2012 to 15 percent in 2013.

In this context, the Ministry of Public Health decided to change its approach and use an innovative methodology—the RRI—to try to meet reproductive health and nutrition targets. This approach was based on developing teams of personnel via health centers, and community health workers working together with clear work plans and targets.

In the example of Niger, the RRI approach was implemented in two to three cycles of 100 days annually at the level of health centers with technical support from their respective districts. This approach was so successful in achieving the identified targets that the government of Niger rated RRI as one of the top innovations in its national health plan in 2017.

- **Global Objective** Increase the number of
  women using modern methods of contraception

  - **Technical and/or Socie Cultural Challenges**
    How to encourage women to go into health
    centers that are integrated with family planning?

    - **Domain of Result**:
      Act within the 5 health districts; strengthen
      collaboration with religious leaders, traditional
      relays, midwives, and NGOs.

    - **Refinement Questions:**
      Which women should we target?
      Should we focus on a specific sector?
      Are there adapted (socieaultural, religious)
      challenges on which to focus?
      What will be the success indicator?
      How many teams to mobilize?

      - **RRI Performance Objective** Increase the number of new
        users (married women or women aged 15 to 49) of modern
        contraception methods from 139,542 (30.26%) to 165,573
        (35.90%), which represents an increase of 26,031 (5.64%)
        from October 7, 2016, to January 29, 2017, across all the
        health districts in the Dosso region.

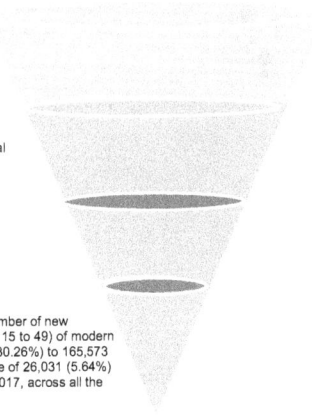

Figure 5.2 Objectives established for the project in Niger

Adapted from 'Guide national pour l'application de l'approche par les résultats rapides
(RRI)',Republique du Niger, Ministère de la santé publique, 2017

One of the main reasons for this success was the focus on establishing
high-performing teams.[†] Referring back to the framework proposed in
this book, there were three main conditions underpinning the work of
these high-performing teams that were crucial for the initiative's success.
I highlight them here:

- Establishing Specific, Achievable Objectives : The funnel
  diagram shown in Figure 5.2 illustrates how the team set
  specific, achievable objectives within a 100-day time frame
  to address the technical and socio-cultural challenges in
  increasing family planning uptake and increase the number of
  women using contraception. This provided the team a clear
  direction but also a sense of urgency to achieve results in a
  short period of time

[†] It is important to mention here that while developing high-performing teams
is crucial for success, it was not the only factor for success in Niger. Effective
results required, for instance, proactive support from leadership and methodical
process support from a coach. This includes identifying root causes of problems
and analyzing actor dynamics during periodic monitoring sessions.

The concept of urgency is fascinating to me and can be a powerful motivator in driving successful initiatives, as seen in various case studies. For instance, while reading Elon Musk's biography,[1] I was particularly struck by his relentless sense of urgency. Although this urgency led to setting seemingly unrealistic deadlines, it also had the effect of unleashing extraordinary potential and drive within his teams. This shows that, with clear objectives and a palpable sense of urgency, initiatives like those in Niger can achieve significant momentum and success.

- Clear Accountability Structure: Teams had a clear accountability structure, with defined roles and responsibilities. This clarity was instrumental in driving the project's success.

  Coming back to the indicator on contraception, work plans were developed in the district with a group of milestones, targets, and a responsible member. Then, for each milestone—for instance, community mobilization strengthened for family planning (FP)—there was a set of specific underlying activities, each with specific results (see Figure 5.3 for an example).

- Empowering Teams to Make Decisions: Teams were empowered to make decisions and take action, fostering a

Milestones	Deliverables	Responsible
Enhanced Service Provision	85% of new FP acceptors admitted, 100% of women find services available	-
Agent Capacity Strengthened in FP	12 health agents and 50 relays trained in FP	-
Community Mobilization Strengthened for FP	85% of new FP acceptors admitted	-

Activities	Results
Conduct 2 awareness sessions per week in 30 villages	840 sessions held
Organize 4 group discussions per week at 3 high schools	56 discussions held
Organize 2 sermons per week at 2 mosques	26 sermons held
Conduct 14 advocacy sessions per week across 4 large villages	784 advocacy sessions held
Provide 10 individual counseling sessions per day, 70 per week	980 counselling sessions held

Figure 5.3 *Accountability template for the project in Niger*

Adapted from 'Guide national pour l'application de l'approchepar les résultats rapides (RRI)', Republique du Niger, Ministèrede la sant. publique, 2017

Activities	Results	
Conduct 2 awareness sessions per week in 30 villages	840 sessions held	Team innovation: include the husbands and religious chiefs in the sessions
Organize 4 group discussions per week at 3 high schools	56 discussions held	
Organize 2 sermons per week at 2 mosques	26 sermons held	
Conduct 14 advocacy sessions per week across 4 large villages	784 advocacy sessions held	
Provide 10 individual counselling sessions per day, 70 per week	980 counselling sessions held	

Figure 5.4 Accountability template used for spurring innovation for the project in Niger

Source: Developed by the author

sense of ownership and creativity. This freedom, coupled with a clear accountability structure, ensured that each team member was fully invested in the project's success, directly impacting the efficiency of health plan implementation.

What we are highlighting here aligns with the framework we are proposing in this manuscript; the approach to developing teams in Niger struck a balance between well-defined structure (i.e., accountability and clear roles) and the freedom to take initiative. This was key to the project's success.

For instance, as shown in Figure 5.4 a team member in one district realized that the awareness sessions part of the community mobilization were not very effective, as only women were participating (in many villages in Niger, the role of the man is still unfortunately fairly dominant). This meant that even if women participated in awareness campaigns, they were not changing their behavior (using contraception or feeding their children better) because men were the ones making decisions. So, the team member decided to include men and religious chiefs in the awareness campaigns, showing the advantages for the whole family of using contraception. This had a highly positive impact on the whole campaign.

Similarly, in another project in Tunisia, I was asked to support the government in an initiative financed by bilateral donors to improve the patient experience in a hospital in Tunis.

After the 2011 revolution, Tunisia faced significant pressure to implement reforms and demonstrate progress. This urgency was compounded by regional disparities, problems with service accessibility, and quality concerns that spanned across service culture, corruption, and the general difficulty citizens faced in accessing services. These challenges affected both the public-facing (front office) and administrative (back office) aspects of service delivery, contributing to a deteriorating perception of Tunisian public administration and a notable disengagement among citizens.

Our research showed that, in the health sector, for instance, several critical issues emerged:

- Widespread dissatisfaction among citizens regarding health care services;
- The government's challenges in delivering concrete and meaningful improvements;
- A lack of actionable data to guide reforms and enhancements.
- In collaboration with the Tunisian government, we embarked on a project aimed at enhancing patient experiences at a hospital in Tunis using a novel approach called "the customer journey."

As Figure 5.5 illustrates, this methodology was specifically chosen to understand the complexities that patients face during their health care interactions by unpacking the patient journey (i.e. patient needs and activities), providing a detailed view of their experiences (i.e. expections for the service and their emotional state). Our short-term goals were to identify opportunities for impactful changes in the patient experience, involve citizens directly in pinpointing problems and cocreating innovative solutions, and test these solutions in a real-world setting. Starting with one hospital, we aimed to refine the solutions and enhance overall service quality and patient satisfaction.

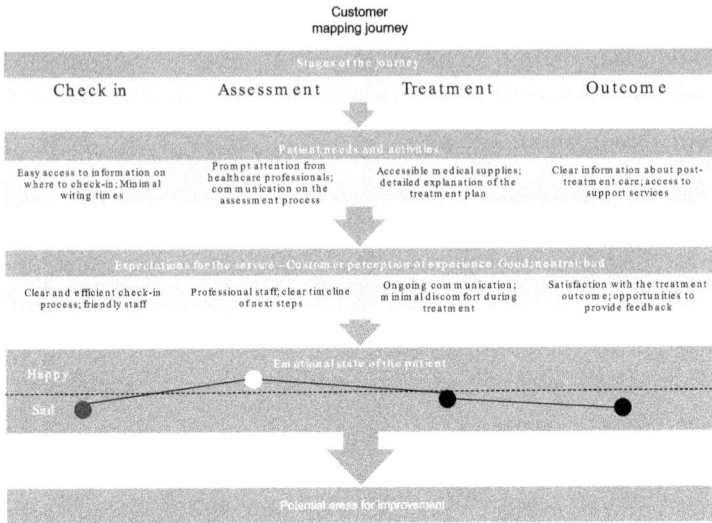

Figure 5.5 Customer Mapping Journey

Source: Developed by the author

Similar to the project in Niger, for this project, we decided to focus significant efforts on establishing a high-performing team within one ministry, setting a precedent we hoped would inspire and catalyze change across other departments.

Key strategies employed to build this high-performing team included:

- Understanding Organizational Dynamics: Recognizing the existing traditional hierarchies and rigid protocols within the government department, noting their impact on motivation.
- Creating an Enabling Environment: Securing support from the director, which allowed us to experiment with new methodologies, embodying the "freedom" aspect of our approach. This is particularly important in more "traditional organizations."
- Team Selection and Structuring: Ensuring we had the right people in the team. This process was tailored to leverage the team members' strengths and interests, promoting pair work to foster collaboration, thus establishing "structure."

- Encouraging Innovation and Experimentation: Providing team members enough room to innovate and experiment, incorporating check-in templates that provided space for noting innovative contributions, reinforcing the "freedom" aspect.
- Defining Responsibilities and Accountability: Clearly delineating team responsibilities and establishing an accountability structure aligned with the project vision to ensure clarity and direction.
- Emphasizing Achievable Results: Focusing on concrete and achievable results to drive progress and maintain momentum.
- Leveraging Project Management and Collaborative Tools: Utilizing productivity and project management tools such as Trello and Slack to streamline workflow and enhance team coordination.
- Meeting Deadlines With Firmness: Paying sufficient attention on how to enforce deadlines with determination, instilling a sense of urgency and commitment to timely delivery among team members.
- Working Fast and Decisively: Prioritizing rapid decision-making and action, in order to navigate and, where possible, circumvent government bureaucracy, accelerating project execution.

At the end of this project, we managed to achieve concrete results to improve the patient experience, such as developing a better signage and communication system for the emergency room in the hospital, as this was a major problem from the patient's point of view.

However, the most rewarding outcome to me was witnessing the excitement and interest of the officials in embracing a new, empowering way of working and inspiring other teams in the ministry to adopt the same approaches and methodologies we had used to build a high-performing team. Interestingly enough, this illustrates a crucial point: significant organizational change doesn't always need to start at the top with senior management or a CEO—indeed, the team we had created in Tunisia was made of middle-level managers as changemakers.

As Simon Sinek points out,[‡] impactful change can indeed begin at any level within an organization—sometimes you do have to wait for the CEO or senior management to bring about change in the organization. When you start with your own team and set an example, the positive results can inspire other teams to follow suit, demonstrating that you don't need to be in a high-level position to make a real difference.

Lessons From Personal Experience: High-Performing Teams in Start-Up Organizations

My experience with start-up organizations in France also provides an interesting perspective on applying the principles of balancing freedom and structure to develop high-performing teams. Whether involved in business development or establishing an internal coaching program, I consistently applied these principles.

In one notable instance, I was working for a growing start-up focused on business development, specifically trying to expand the start-up by opening new spaces for a co-working café. Creativity in idea generation and implementation was crucial, as we aimed to disrupt the market and find innovative solutions. We emphasized empowering team members to initiate and propose creative ideas. However, unlike my work in more traditional settings, I found it necessary to place greater emphasis on establishing a clear structure around the team rather than focusing solely on autonomy.

This meant setting specific targets, delineating roles and responsibilities, and ensuring clear accountability. This structured approach led to

---

[‡] Simon Sineck suggests that impactful change can begin at any level within an organization—sometimes you do have to wait for the CEO or senior management to bring about change in the organization. By starting with your own team and setting an example, the positive results can inspire other teams to follow suit, demonstrating that you don't need to be in a high-level position to make a real difference. Sinek, Simon. 2023. Human Capital Leadership Institute, Presentation. Available at www.linkedin.com/feed/update/urn:li:activity:7187123548585406465/.

better coordination, more effective project management, and ultimately, a successful expansion that met our strategic goals.

Another example I'd like to mention is my work with a start-up testing a new knowledge-management platform for a university in the United States. The platform aimed to match students with relevant courses that might interest them and connect students with professors and peers who shared common interests. This project required a delicate balance of freedom and structure to succeed. One of the most innovative aspects of this project was developing an algorithm to enhance the matching process. Initially, the team faced challenges in ensuring that the algorithm could accurately pair students with courses and people based on diverse criteria such as academic interests, extracurricular activities, and social media profiles.

During a brainstorming session, a team member proposed incorporating machine learning techniques to analyze patterns in student behavior and preferences. This idea was initially met with skepticism due to its complexity, but the team was given the freedom to explore it further. Over several weeks, they experimented with different models and datasets, refining the algorithm to improve its accuracy. The breakthrough came when a team member suggested integrating a natural language processing component to analyze students' social media posts and online activity. By understanding the context and sentiment behind these posts, the algorithm could better predict students' interests and academic inclinations. This innovation significantly improved the platform's matching capabilities, making it more intuitive and user-friendly.

While the team had the autonomy to innovate, it was crucial to have a structured framework to keep the project on track. We implemented regular check-ins and progress reports to ensure milestones were met and maintained a defined roadmap to manage the project's complexity. Clear guidelines for each development phase helped balance creativity with accountability, ensuring that the team stayed focused on the platform's goals.

As a result, the platform not only matched students with courses that aligned with their academic interests but also connected them with professors and peers who shared similar passions and goals. This holistic approach fostered a more engaged and collaborative learning environment, enhancing the overall educational experience.

Distilling Insights From High-Performing Teams: Key Strategies Employed

Both in traditional organizations and start-ups, the agile equilibrium between freedom and structure is essential for nurturing high-performing teams, even if the balance might be adjusted according to the specific challenges and dynamics of each environment.

Let's reiterate the three main conditions for team performance that are valuable for organizations that we have just mentioned in the examples from traditional and startup organizations:

- Providing Purpose and Clear Direction: A shared purpose serves as the main direction for the team, guiding decision-making and aligning efforts. When team members understand how their work contributes to the overarching goals, they are more motivated and engaged. Clear direction also includes setting expectations and providing the vision needed to inspire action toward common objectives.
- Creating a Clear Accountability Structure: Accountability ensures that responsibilities are well-defined and understood, allowing for effective tracking of progress and outcomes. This structure doesn't just clarify who is responsible for what; it also establishes a system for feedback and support, enabling individuals and teams to understand their performance and areas for improvement. Such clarity is crucial for empowerment, as it allows employees to take ownership of their roles and contributions without ambiguity.
- Giving Team Members Enough Room to Take Initiatives: Empowerment is largely about trust—trusting team members to take initiatives and make decisions within their scope of work. By giving them the room to innovate and take calculated risks, organizations can foster a culture of creativity and problem-solving. However, this autonomy must be

balanced with the right level of support and guidance to ensure that these initiatives align with the team's goals and values.

While these conditions are fundamental for a team's performance, the additional critical dimension is understanding the specific context in which a team operates. This involves considering factors such as the type of organization (e.g., a start-up or a traditional firm) and other situational variables. For example, while working with a start-up in Paris, I realized that, despite the ample freedom to innovate, what the team needed most was structure. Conversely, in Tunisia, understanding the constraints that affected the team's ability to innovate and take initiatives was crucial. This contextual awareness highlights the fact that, while structure and freedom are necessary, their application must be tailored to fit the unique environmental and organizational conditions of each team. This nuanced understanding is pivotal for developing high-performing teams. As we have been repeating, too much structure can stifle creativity and initiative, while too much freedom can lead to chaos and misalignment. To achieve this, conducting a quick diagnostic of the team's and organization's specific context can guide you on how to best balance these elements.

How Great Organizations Apply the Agile Equilibrium in Teams

In exploring how high-performing teams operate within great companies, I've noticed something interesting that I would like to highlight here. *Whether it's decision-making, planning, or organizing team meetings, these companies have crafted specific practices and even rituals that balance team autonomy with structured approaches.* This balance not only allows teams the freedom to chart their own course but also ensures they stay aligned with the broader goals of the organization, creating an environment where independence and strategic direction harmoniously coexist.

Let's now unpack this.

One of the most common and sometimes difficult things in a team setting is, for instance, to take decisions.

Streamlining Decision-Making and Empowerment

Great companies have developed structured processes for decision-making while simultaneously empowering employees. Here are some general rules and protocols these companies use:

- Implement Deadlines: Setting clear deadlines to ensure the decision-making process is efficient and concludes within a set time frame.
- Encourage Healthy Debate: Encouraging arguing or disagreeing as it is beneficial. This ensures that diverse viewpoints are considered, leading to more robust decisions.
- Demand Full Engagement: Requiring full engagement from all participants. If you attend a meeting, be fully present. Active participation ensures that all voices are heard and maximizes the effectiveness of the gathering.
- Practice Transparency: Ensuring decision-making processes are transparent, allowing team members to understand how and why decisions are made.
- Use Data-Driven Insights: Supporting decisions with data and analytics. This guides thinking and helps minimize bias.

While providing some structure around decision-making, great companies also empower and encourage employees to take decisions, even in situations of ambiguity. For instance, at Amazon, Jeff Bezos says that "most decisions should probably be made with somewhere around 70 percent of the information you wish you had. If you wait for 90 percent, in most cases, you're probably being slow. Plus, either way, you need to be good at quickly recognizing and correcting bad decisions. If you're good at course correcting, being wrong may be less costly than you think, whereas being slow is going to be expensive for sure."[2]

In this approach to empowerment, some companies try to decentralize the process of decision-making. At Semco, important decisions are made in a collegiate manner, or even through companywide votes. An illustrative example is the collective decision to select a new plant for the marine division, demonstrating an unwavering commitment to participatory management. Such practices not only decentralize decision-making but also deeply involve employees in the company's operational and strategic directions, making the achievements truly collective.

What I also found interesting is that great companies, such as Buurtzorg, take an extra step by integrating decision-making coaching into their onboarding processes. This approach equips employees with the skills needed to navigate the complexities of their roles from the outset, fostering a sense of empowerment and initiative.

Rather than providing some generic principles to employees and team members, some great companies have devised specific decision-making processes, such as the "advice process," to make decisions without getting stuck looking for consensus or a quick decision process. This approach allows any individual to make decisions after consulting with those significantly impacted and those with relevant expertise. The objective isn't to reach a compromise but to harness collective wisdom for the best possible action. This process underscores the fact that advice is just that—advice. The final decision rests with the initiator, promoting a culture where power is shared, and initiative is encouraged.

Let's try to illustrate how the advice process works in an example from Morning Star, a company that primarily produces tomato-based products, and is known for being the largest tomato processor in the world.

A few years ago, prior to the widespread use of internal social networks, Chris Rufer, the founder and CEO of Morning Star, recognized the need for a new strategic direction within the company. To facilitate this, he crafted a memo outlining his proposed strategy, and distributed it to all employees. He then invited everyone to a companywide meeting, which was conducted via videoconference across various locations. During the meeting, Chris shared his ideas and the motivations behind them. He concluded by encouraging all employees to contact him directly after the meeting with any questions, concerns, or feedback regarding his plans, emphasizing open communication and collaboration.[§]

Contrary to the binary view of decision-making as either authoritarian or consensus-driven, the advice process offers a third way. It empowers

---

§ https://reinventingorganizationswiki.com/en/theory/decision-making/.

the decision-maker to act with autonomy while considering varied inputs, without necessitating unanimous agreement. This method avoids the pitfalls of consensus, where decisions can be stalled by the need for universal approval. Instead, it places responsibility and ownership firmly in the hands of the decision-maker, who, equipped with diverse perspectives, can proceed with conviction and accountability.

The advice process fosters several benefits, as it builds community through shared involvement and information, promotes humility by acknowledging the need for others' input, facilitates learning through hands-on decision-making, leads to better decisions by leveraging collective insights, and introduces an element of fun, mirroring the collaborative spirit of team sports.

Implementing the advice process involves recognizing an issue, consulting to formulate a proposal, seeking advice from those affected (and with expertise), and then, with this advice in hand, making an informed decision. The scope of consultation varies with the decision's impact, from informal discussions to broader solicitations of input, and possibly involving digital platforms for larger groups.

Certainly, there are also other practices that some companies have developed to structure the decision-making processes. Some companies have developed innovative methods to enhance their decision-making processes. For example, Bridgewater Associates, one of the biggest hedge funds in the world, as mentioned earlier, employs a unique approach known as "believability weighting."[3] This process involves evaluating the opinions of team members based on their credibility, which is determined by their track record and expertise related to the decision at hand.

When Bridgewater makes significant investment decisions, they don't just count votes; instead, they weigh each vote based on how believable each team member has proven to be in their specific area of expertise. This method ensures that the most informed opinions have a greater impact on the final decision, leading to more accurate and effective outcomes.

Making the Decision-Making Processes Quicker

Great companies not only structure decision-making but also emphasize its rapidity. Speed is crucial in decision-making, especially in dynamic business environments. Recognizing that traditional decision-making can often be time-consuming, *great companies are focusing on how to streamline processes designed for rapid decision-making.* These processes are crafted to expedite approvals and actions, allowing teams to move forward swiftly on projects without the typical delays. This approach not only decentralizes decision-making authority but also significantly reduces the time it takes to make and implement decisions.

Let me give you an example of a quick-decision process that some teams apply at Google Ventures,[4] which includes the following steps:

1. Art Museum: The team start by displaying solution sketches in a row for team review.
2. Heat Map: Individuals silently indicate their preferences with dot stickers.
3. Speed Critique: The group holds a quick discussion highlighting the merits and drawbacks of each solution.
4. Straw Poll: Team members silently vote on their favorite ideas.
5. Supervote: The team members appoint a "decider" who uses large dot stickers to make final selections for prototyping and testing.

By using this approach, teams can make better decisions faster, aligning closely behind a unified direction and significantly enhancing their capacity to innovate and execute efficiently.

The quick decision process is part of the Google's "design sprints," which offer a transformative approach by condensing the development cycle into five days!

Indeed, the traditional project cycle, with its high upfront costs and aversion to failure, often stifles innovation and hampers teams from uniting behind a single vision. This reluctance to experiment with unproven ideas leads to decisions that fail to resonate with users, resulting in uninspired and unsuccessful outcomes.

The sprint developed by Google entails spending the first three days on research and idea development, the fourth on building a testable prototype, and the fifth on gathering user feedback. This approach forces a company to make 60 to 80 percent of product decisions quickly, which is an effective strategy for breaking through indecision and galvanizing teams around a clear vision.

Key steps in the design sprint process include the following:

- Designating a Decider: Identifying a lead decision-maker ensures authority and direction, while voting on this role promotes trust and transparency within the team.
- Setting a Deadline: Utilizing deadlines to motivate progress and prevent stagnation, ensuring that the team remains focused on delivering tangible results to users.
- Going With Your Experience: Trusting in the team's expertise and experience to guide decision-making, allowing for educated guesses and innovative solutions that surpass mere incremental improvements.
- Getting Your Users to Shoot You Down: Rapidly prototyping and seeking user feedback within a day, using tools like Lookback for real-time reactions, ensures the product meets genuine user needs.
- If You Don't Know Next Steps, You Didn't Decide: Ensuring that decisions lead to clear, actionable next steps, avoiding the common pitfall of indecisiveness that slows project momentum.

Effective Project Planning: Empowering Team Members

When it comes to *planning projects and initiatives, the same foundational principles of balancing structure with freedom apply.*

While it's essential to have a structured plan and clear objectives (structure), it's equally important to allow teams the freedom to make adjustments and innovate (freedom). This approach ensures that teams remain aligned with the broader organizational goals while being agile and responsive to changes (see Figure 5.6).

- Why: Create Alignment—The primary goal is to ensure that all team members are working toward common objectives, creating a sense of purpose and direction.

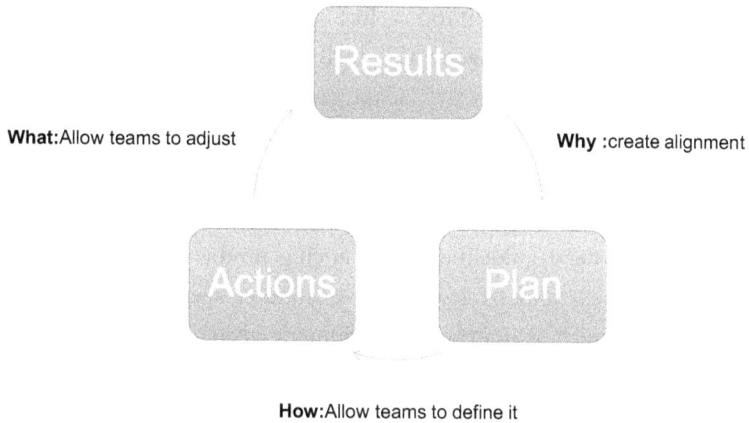

Figure 5.6 Approach to define clear objectives and empower teams to implement and adapt actions

Source: Developed by the author

- How: Allow Teams to Define It—Teams are given the autonomy to define their specific goals and methods, fostering ownership and innovation.
- What: Allow Teams to Adjust—Flexibility is built into the process, allowing teams to adapt their plans and actions as circumstances change.

At Menlo Innovations, for instance, the project planning process is effectively structured, with tools such as cards, origami, and time sheets, empowering the team members to take ownership (freedom) while ensuring that managers provide validation (structure).[5] For example, the employees in the company use physical cards and origami to visually map out project tasks and timelines, making it easier for team members to grasp the scope and sequence of work. They also incorporate time sheets in a way that helps track progress and allocate resources efficiently. This methodical use of visual and tracking tools not only organizes the workflow but also aids in maintaining a transparent and accountable project environment. An illustrative case is how they handled one complex software development project, where using these tools enabled the team to clearly see each phase of development and adjust timelines dynamically, leading to timely project completion and client satisfaction.

Similarly, some organizations like Morning Star adopt a fluid approach to project management, which forgoes rigid master plans in favor of evolving priorities that adapt organically to changing circumstances. This method allows for greater flexibility and responsiveness, so it is particularly well-suited to the dynamic nature of their operations.

For instance, in their tomato processing facilities, project teams might start with a general guideline for enhancing production efficiency but adjust their focus and tactics as they encounter specific challenges or opportunities, such as unexpected equipment advances or shifts in crop yields. This adaptive strategy not only keeps projects aligned with current realities but also encourages innovation and problem-solving on the fly, leading to more effective and tailored outcomes.

This approach extends beyond project development to strategic planning, where the overarching vision and objectives (the "what") are clearly defined, while the methods to achieve them (the "how") are creatively and flexibly determined by the team—an agile strategy.

Empowering Teams Through Flexible Budgeting

In great companies, this flexible planning extends to budgeting and procurement processes, *as teams are given the autonomy to forecast their own budgets without interference from upper management, demonstrating trust in their expertise and judgment.*

At times, great companies implement a structured approach to budgeting when it is directly linked to essential decision-making processes, such as resource coordination or cash flow management. This structure is, however, not rigid, but is designed to provide a framework within which teams can operate effectively. For instance, the practice of making rough forecasts or simple cash flow projections provides a guideline for future activities without imposing unnecessary constraints on teams.

Overall, great companies empower teams by giving them enough room to make budgeting decisions and adjustments.

At Netflix, the flexible planning approach exemplifies an agile equilibrium between freedom and structure; this is particularly evident within their content development teams. This balance is crucial in empowering their teams while ensuring alignment with broader company objectives.

For instance, when producing the hit series *Stranger Things,* the show's creators, the Duffer Brothers, were provided with significant freedom to manage their production budget. Netflix set an initial budget based on the series' scope and expectations, but allowed the creators to make real-time adjustments as needed, to enhance creative output. This flexibility allowed them to allocate additional funds for special effects or to capitalize on unexpected shooting opportunities that would enrich the narrative, without undergoing a lengthy approval process.

This method of entrusting teams to manage their budgets responsibly underscores Netflix's philosophy of prioritizing innovation and quality over strict budgetary controls. It reflects an agile equilibrium where there is enough structure to provide a clear budgetary framework, yet sufficient freedom for creative decision-making. The result is highly successful, original content that resonates with audiences globally, driving subscription growth and reinforcing Netflix's reputation as a pioneer in the entertainment industry. This approach not only accelerates the production process but also unleashes creative potential, allowing teams to produce work that is both visionary and closely aligned with Netflix's brand of pushing creative boundaries.

Fostering Innovation Through Structured Creativity

Great companies understand that fostering creativity requires a blend of structure and freedom. This approach encourages teams to generate creative ideas efficiently while ensuring that these ideas align with the company's strategic goals.

A concrete example of structured creativity in action is the development of the "Keep the Change" program for Bank of America a global design company known for its innovative way of working, IDEO, used.

- Empathize: IDEO's team spent time with various Bank of America customers, observing and interviewing them to understand their savings habits and financial challenges. They discovered that many people wanted to save money but struggled with traditional saving methods.

- Define: Based on their research, IDEO defined the core problem: How might we help people save money effortlessly? They identified key pain points, such as the difficulty of setting aside money regularly and the lack of motivation to save.
- Ideate: IDEO facilitated brainstorming sessions to generate ideas for effortless saving mechanisms. The team used the "Crazy 8s" exercise, among other techniques, to produce a wide range of concepts. One standout idea was to round up purchases to the nearest dollar and transfer the difference into a savings account automatically.
- Prototype: IDEO created low-fidelity prototypes of the "Keep the Change" feature. They developed simple mock-ups of banking interfaces and transaction processes to illustrate how the feature would work. These prototypes allowed the team to visualize the idea and make necessary adjustments.
- Test: The prototypes were tested with real customers to gather feedback. Users were asked to interact with the prototypes and provide their thoughts on the functionality and ease of use. Based on this feedback, IDEO iterated on the design, refining it to better meet user needs.

This process exemplifies how structured creativity can lead to innovative solutions. By following a clear framework and allowing flexibility within each stage, IDEO ensures that their creative efforts are both directed and expansive. The success of the "Keep the Change" program demonstrates the power of this approach, showing how structured creativity can drive creativity and innovation in a real-world context.

Similarly, the Crazy 8 exercise, which we just mentioned, complements this approach by blending structured methodologies with the freedom to explore diverse ideas quickly. Here's an explanation of the exercise, based on the agile equilibrium we are proposing in this book.

Structure of the Crazy 8 Exercise:

- Time-Bound: Participants are given exactly eight minutes to sketch out eight different ideas, allocating one minute per idea. This strict time limit imposes a structured environment that pushes participants to think quickly and efficiently.
- Defined Objective: The exercise starts with a clear, specific challenge or problem statement. This objective provides direction, ensuring that the creative energy of participants is channeled toward relevant and impactful solutions.
- Individual Creativity: Each participant works individually during the sketching phase, which allows for a wide range of ideas to surface without the immediate influence or critique of others. This phase emphasizes freedom, enabling participants to explore diverse thought processes and innovative solutions.

Freedom Within the Crazy 8 Exercise:

- Diverse Ideas: The requirement to produce eight different sketches encourages participants to stretch their imagination and explore varied solutions, including ones that might initially seem unconventional or risky. This aspect of the exercise celebrates creative freedom and the potential for out-of-the-box thinking.
- Iterative Exploration: Participants are free to build upon, refine, or completely change direction with each new sketch. This iterative process allows for the exploration of multiple facets of the problem and potential solutions, embodying the freedom to pivot and adapt ideas based on evolving thoughts.
- Inclusive Participation: By encouraging every participant to contribute ideas, the exercise democratizes the creative process. This inclusivity fosters a sense of ownership and empowerment among team members, allowing for a richer tapestry of perspectives and solutions.

Structuring Meetings for Maximum Efficiency

The Crazy 8 exercise highlights how structuring creative processes can significantly enhance productivity, a principle that extends seamlessly to organizing meetings.

I remember working for traditional organizations where meetings were often characterized by one-way communication from managers, a lack of decisive action, and attendees arriving unprepared, due to competing commitments.

Conversely, when working with some start-ups I realized that we would hold some meetings that lacked a defined agenda and structure, leading to inefficiency.

Great companies have developed protocols for organizing and conducting meetings that not only empower employees but also ensure productive and decisive discussions.

For example, Buurtzorg hosts meetings only when necessary, underpinned by clear rules such as a single decision-maker, defined objectives, a shared agenda, and limited attendance to maintain focus and efficiency. This approach decentralizes decision-making by empowering employees with clear responsibilities, thus minimizing the need for excessive meetings.

Amazon exemplifies a distinct meeting culture, especially with its innovative use of written memos:[6]

- The Six-Page Memo: Amazon initiates meetings with attendees quietly reading a detailed six-page memo, which is the result of weeks of collaborative and iterative writing. This memo thoroughly addresses the meeting topic, ensuring a deep, shared understanding.
- Narrative Over Slides: Preferring narrative memos to slide presentations, Amazon believes that structured narratives demand clearer thinking and foster more insightful discussions.
- Collaborative Writing Process: The memo's development involves numerous drafts and diverse input, guaranteeing a comprehensive perspective on the issue at hand.

- Premeeting Preparation: The memo is distributed in advance, with time allocated at the start of the meeting for reading, ensuring that all participants are equally informed and prepared.
- Emphasis on Detail: This approach roots discussions in detailed narrative and data analysis, promoting a thorough examination of the topics.
- Informed Decision-Making: The detailed preparatory work and discussion help in making well-informed decisions, grounded in collective understanding and consensus.

What happens is that great companies (and teams within) end up organizing less meetings than traditional organizations, as they focus on those meetings that are truly necessary, with only the attendees who are supposed to participate.

One reason for this is that by empowering employees to make decisions independently, great companies reduce the necessity for managerial oversight of meetings. For instance, in the case of FAVI, if an employee has the autonomy to implement a change directly, the need for meetings to address issues or solutions is significantly diminished. This empowerment model, often referred to as reverse delegation, expects frontline teams and operators to handle all tasks except for those that they specifically escalate.

Another reason is that, as transparency and communication is central to great companies (as we will see later), there is less need to have meetings to share information, which is needed in traditional organizations where information is often filtered between different levels of the chain of command, and employees do not have access to all the relevant data.

Therefore, by ensuring that information flows freely and responsibilities are clearly defined, these organizations foster an environment where meetings are purposeful, productive, and conducive to fostering innovation.

Embracing Self-Reflection and Continuous Learning

Another thing I've found very interesting in great companies, which is essential in building high-performing teams, is the practice of self-reflection and continuous learning.

Teams within these organizations regularly dedicate time to self-reflection. For example, teams using the SCRUM methodology[¶] do not merely focus on the problems at hand, but also consistently evaluate their collaboration dynamics. They utilize check-in templates that prompt simple yet essential questions about their teamwork and processes. This practice of continuous internal assessment is crucial in maintaining their agility and enhancing overall team performance.

In the realm of high-performing teams, continuous feedback loops play a pivotal role, extending beyond collective processes to foster individual growth and self-improvement. This dual focus on team dynamics and personal development underscores a holistic approach to performance enhancement that is prevalent in many great companies. These organizations recognize that the path to sustained high performance is paved with ongoing feedback and the constant pursuit of excellence, not just at the team level but also at the individual level.

For instance, Google is renowned for its robust peer review system, which exemplifies this concept. This system isn't just about assessing performance; it's deeply integrated into the professional development of each employee. Through structured peer feedback, individuals receive actionable insights not only about their contributions to team projects but also about their personal competencies and areas for growth. This continuous loop of feedback ensures that learning and development are integral to

---

¶ Scrum is an agile framework designed to enhance team collaboration on complex projects. It organizes work into small, manageable iterations known as sprints, typically lasting two to four weeks. During these sprints, teams work through a set of functions from a backlog that defines the work needed for the project. Scrum encourages regular updates on progress through daily meetings and end-of-sprint reviews, facilitating adaptability and quick pivots in response to changing project requirements. The framework is led by roles such as the Scrum Master and Product Owner, who help maintain the process and prioritize tasks, respectively.

the daily work experience, facilitating a culture of continuous improvement and adaptation.

Another exemplary model of this approach is Adobe's "check-in" framework. Moving away from traditional annual performance reviews, Adobe has implemented a more dynamic system where managers and team members engage in regular, informal discussions about performance, priorities, and personal development goals. This ongoing dialogue ensures that feedback is timely and relevant, allowing for immediate adjustments and fostering a proactive attitude toward personal and professional growth. The check-in system not only enhances engagement by making feedback a regular part of the work experience but it also aligns individual goals with team objectives, thereby driving overall organizational success.

Throughout my experience with projects in both the private and public sectors, indeed I've noticed a common oversight; even if we would organize many meetings (sometimes far too many!) to focus strongly on project progress and potential obstacles, we neglected to assess how we would function as a team. It's crucial not only to discuss what challenges we are facing but also to evaluate our communication, collaboration, and overall team dynamics.

To address this in my own projects and building on the examples of great companies, I introduced a practice of incorporating check-in questions into regular team meetings on how we collaborated as a team. These questions are designed to "take the temperature" of team collaboration, asking simple yet profound questions about how team members feel they are working together. This practice has enabled teams to not only tackle project-related issues but also to enhance their working relationships and continuously improve their collective efficiency. Figure 5.7. illustrates how team collaboration questions can be integrated into check-in meetings alongside project-focused questions to foster both operational success and a positive team environment.

Cultivating a Team Culture of Experimentation and Embracing Failure

Building on the practices of self-reflection and continuous learning, embracing a culture that values experimentation and the inevitable

What did we learn?

About the problem we are addressing:	Have our understanding of the problem's scope and nature evolved? Are there underlying assumptions we need to revisit?
About the strategies we're implementing:	Which strategies have been most effective, and what have we learned from them? Are there any unintended consequences or learnings from these strategies that we need to address?
About our operational context:	How have changes in our operational environment affected our project? What shifts in stakeholder attitudes or regulatory landscapes have impacted our work?
About working as a team:	What strengths and weaknesses in our team dynamics have emerged? How effectively are we communicating and collaborating under pressure?

Figure 5.7 *Example of a team check-in template including some key learning and self-reflection questions*

Source: Developed by the author

lessons learned from failure is integral to cultivating high-performing teams. This approach is encapsulated in the philosophy of "win or learn," where failure is not seen as a setback but as an essential component of the learning process.

In the tech industry, this is often formalized through the practice of conducting "postmortems" after projects. These sessions are dedicated to dissecting what went well and what didn't, without a focus on blame. The key here is to understand and document the lessons to improve future efforts. This type of reflective practice is crucial for continuous improvement, but is noticeably absent or underutilized in many traditional sectors, both public and private.

For example, in my own work, whether in start-up environments or at times in more structured corporate settings, I've tried to integrate this "postmortem" process.

Earlier, I gave you the example of a new marketing strategy we were trying to develop in a start-up that initially did not meet its targets. Instead of writing it off as a failure, we conducted a detailed postmortem that revealed crucial insights about our market assumptions and outreach tactics. These insights directly informed our next strategy, leading to a successful campaign on the subsequent try.

This concept draws from the Kaizen philosophy, which is rooted in the belief that continuous, incremental improvement adds up to substantial change over time. Each little change, each experiment, whether it fails or succeeds, contributes to the broader goal of long-term improvement.

Building Trust Through Transparency and Communication

Something that we have mentioned in our discussion on great companies and we hinted again here when discussing performing teams is the critical importance of transparency and communication as foundational elements. Transparency is the "condition sine qua non" other principles can be applied effectively.

For instance, we recently discussed the importance for teams to discuss and learn from failures. This would not be possible in an environment where transparency and communication are not practiced.

Indeed, transparency and communication are not just operational tactics but are fundamental to the ethos of high-performing teams. They build a foundation of trust across the organization.

All great companies I came across, therefore, preach about those elements.

This commitment to transparency and trust is underpinned by research, such as Google's Project Aristotle,[7] which identified psychological safety as a critical factor in team effectiveness. Establishing norms around vulnerability and trust, conflict resolution, and feedback contributes to a culture where team members feel it is safe to express dissent, suggest changes, and collectively decide on next steps to resolve conflicts.

Great companies prioritize trust over mere performance, echoing the sentiments of thought leaders like Simon Sinek, who notes that teams, including those as critical as Navy SEALs, value trustworthiness even above individual performance metrics.[8] This emphasis on psychological safety[9] and trust over sheer performance highlights the nuanced team dynamics that characterize great companies, fostering a culture where innovation and collaboration thrive.

A compelling illustration of the effective interplay between trust and honesty in team dynamics is exemplified by the Pixar Braintrust, as introduced by its former president Ed Catmull.[10]** This innovative approach significantly contributes to nurturing creativity, collaboration, and excellence at Pixar.

In practice, the Pixar Braintrust brings together directors, writers, and other creatives from within the company to review and critique ongoing projects at pivotal stages.

An example of how this works can be seen in the development of *Toy Story 3*. During an early Braintrust meeting, the team faced a narrative challenge: the story wasn't resonating emotionally with the audience in the way they had intended. The meeting was characterized by openness, with participants encouraged to share their unfiltered opinions about the film's storyline and character development.

In this environment of trust and candor, feedback was given directly but with a clear focus on problem-solving rather than criticism for criticism's sake. For instance, one Braintrust member pointed out that the emotional connection with Woody's character felt weakened in the current storyline. This observation was not perceived as a personal attack, but as a valuable insight aimed at improving the film. Because the Braintrust operates without a hierarchical structure, suggestions and critiques are received as helpful advice from peers who are genuinely invested in the project's success.

The directors and writers listened to the Braintrust's feedback and returned to the drawing board, armed with fresh perspectives. They reworked the storyline to deepen the emotional stakes of the film, enhancing the connection between Woody and the audience. This iterative process, fueled by the Braintrust's culture of candor and trust, ensured that *Toy Story 3* was a critically acclaimed success, demonstrating the practical impact of these principles on Pixar's creative output.

** I To learn more about 'focused time blocks', see Newport, Cal. 2016. Deep Work: Rules for Focused Success in a Distracted World (Grand Central Publishing), page 226.

Leveraging Operational Tools to Enhance Communication and Trust

As we discuss the importance of communication and trust in creating high-performing teams, it's clear that choosing and using the right tools is also crucial to practice those elements. We already mentioned project management tools such as Trello for the example in Tunisia. These technologies should not only facilitate efficient workflow, but should also enhance transparency and build trust among team members. The key is to implement these tools in a way that supports the team's natural dynamics without imposing overly rigid structures that could dampen motivation and creativity.

Tools such as Asana and Trello offer frameworks that can enhance organizational efficiency by providing clear visibility of tasks, responsibilities, and deadlines. These tools enable teams to track project progress in real-time, assign tasks dynamically, and adjust priorities as needed, which aligns well with the principle of structured flexibility. By clearly outlining who is responsible for what and by when, these platforms help ensure that everyone on the team is aligned, which is critical for maintaining both accountability and a sense of collective purpose.

However, while these tools offer numerous benefits, they also present challenges. The structure provided by such platforms can sometimes be perceived as constraining, particularly when team members feel compelled to fit their workflows into predefined templates or reporting structures. This can potentially stifle creativity and initiative, if it is not managed carefully. Additionally, the reliance on digital tools for communication and collaboration can sometimes lead to an overemphasis on asynchronous communication, possibly undermining the richness of the direct, face-to-face interactions that foster deeper trust and understanding.

Microsoft Teams, another widely used collaboration platform, exemplifies the way that technology can support both structured interactions and spontaneous communication. With features that support both scheduled meetings and chat-based, informal interactions, Microsoft Teams can help maintain the balance between necessary structure and the freedom for more organic, creative exchanges. This dual capability is essential for teams who thrive on quick collaboration, but also need to document and structure their workflows rigorously.

While these tools can be very effective, their success depends on the overall environment of the team and the organization in which they are developed and implemented. As we have repeatedly seen, all dimensions in the agile framework are indeed interconnected. Therefore, the implementation of these tools must be accompanied by a supportive culture that values transparency, accountability, and open communication. This ensures that the tools enhance rather than hinder the team's performance and creativity.

Conclusion

High-performing teams balance freedom and structure, aligning their actions with a clear purpose while fostering an environment that encourages creativity and initiative. The principles that drive successful organizations are equally crucial at the team level.

As we have seen from the personal examples I provided, the essence of a high-performing team lies in its ability to combine a well-defined mission and clear accountability with the flexibility to innovate. Teams need specific, achievable objectives that provide direction. Clear roles and responsibilities are essential for maintaining accountability, ensuring that everyone knows their contributions and how they align with the broader goals.

Great companies have developed specific protocols to balance team autonomy with structured approaches, thereby enhancing team performance. They achieve this by organizing decision-making processes, planning, budgeting methodologies, and even structuring how meetings are conducted. These protocols and structures don't constrain employees; instead, they empower them by providing clear boundaries within which they can take initiatives and be more creative.

Similarly, to our discussion at the organizational level, high-performing teams foster environments where transparency and trust are fundamental principles, as illustrated in the Agile Equilibrium Framework.

This framework is not just applicable to organizations and teams, but also offers a valuable lens for enhancing individual productivity. The principles of agile equilibrium can help individuals structure their time and tasks in a way that balances sufficient structure with the necessary freedom for creativity and flexibility (see next).

CHAPTER 6

The Agile Equilibrium at the Individual Level

Balancing Structure and Freedom in Personal Workflow

Navigating multiple assignments simultaneously has compelled me to develop, test, and refine effective systems tailored to my diverse workload. This journey toward trying to optimize personal productivity involved a significant transformation from a traditional structured work environment to a more flexible freelance model.

In a conventional setting, my days were strictly scheduled, beginning at 9 a.m. sharp and filled with back-to-back meetings. This rigid structure, though seemingly organized, often fragmented my day—splitting my focus between analytical tasks and incessant emails. Directives on time management and task prioritization were abundant, but they left little room for autonomy, leading to fatigue and decreased productivity within, at times, just a few hours of work.

Shifting to freelancing brought a new set of challenges. The freedom to devise my own schedule was liberating yet daunting.

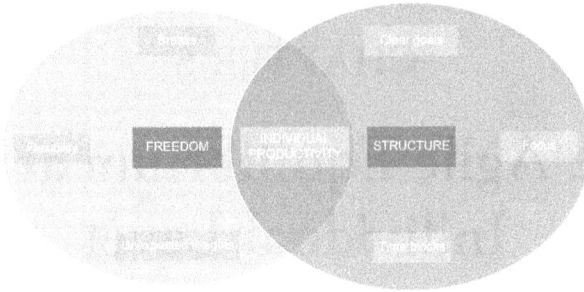

Figure 6.1 Individual productivity

Source: Developed by the author

Without the external structure of an office environment, I initially struggled with inefficiencies. My days lacked rhythm, and I found it difficult to harness the right motivation and focus.

To navigate these challenges, *I began to craft a personalized approach that balanced structure with the necessary freedom to foster individual creativity and drive* (see Figure 6.1).

This strategy is rooted in the principles of agile equilibrium, which prioritize adaptability and structured flexibility.

- Adopting Planning Tools: I embraced digital tools such as Asana and Google Calendar to meticulously organize tasks and deadlines. These tools serve as the backbone of my daily and monthly planning, allowing me to visualize progress and adjust plans dynamically.
- Setting Monthly Goals and Deliverables: Establishing clear monthly targets was pivotal. Instead of vague objectives, I specified what I intended to accomplish, breaking this down into weekly and daily tasks. This structured approach ensured steady progress and provided clear benchmarks for success.
- Prioritizing Work and Focus: I identified key tasks that needed attention each day. Lesser priorities were relegated or removed to minimize distractions. This focus is crucial, especially when managing diverse projects that require different levels of engagement and creativity.

- Allocating Time Based on Productivity Peaks: After recognizing that my concentration peaks in the morning, I scheduled demanding tasks during these hours. Meetings and collaborative efforts were set for the afternoon when my individual productivity naturally dipped, but my collaborative energy peaked.
- Monitoring Energy and Attention: I adopted a mindful approach to work, tuning into my energy levels and attention span throughout the day. This self-awareness allowed me to adapt my workload dynamically—tackling complex problems when I felt most alert and shifting to less demanding tasks as my energy waned.
- Incorporating Regular Breaks: Integrating breaks into my schedule proved essential for mental rejuvenation and creativity. These aren't mere pauses but crucial periods for idea incubation and problem-solving.

The integration of LLMs has dramatically enhanced my productivity by streamlining content creation, data analysis, and automated task management. LLMs, such as ChatGPT, assist in generating high-quality text, offering contextual insights, and automating repetitive tasks that otherwise consume considerable time. This not only speeds up the process but also maintains a high standard of accuracy and creativity, allowing me to allocate more time to strategic thinking and less on routine tasks.

Strategic Time Management

In adopting agile principles for individual productivity, one of the most critical factors I've honed in on is the strategic use of time. The essence of the Agile Equilibrium Framework, when it is applied to personal work habits, lies in the effective management of time. This process focuses on optimizing periods of high productivity while allowing flexibility to foster creativity. Through this approach, I've crafted a workflow that aligns with my natural rhythms and professional demands. This method grants me the flexibility to engage my creativity fully, while the structured aspects ensure that I meet my objectives and deadlines reliably. This kind of balance is vital for handling diverse and fluctuating project demands, particularly in freelance environments, where self-direction is key.

An example of this balanced approach's effectiveness came during a complex evaluation project I spearheaded. This project required a blend of creative synthesis and rigorous detail orientation. Here's how I applied my time management strategy:

- Planning With Precision: Before diving into the project, I outlined the major milestones and estimated the time required for each phase. This initial planning phase was crucial for setting realistic expectations and deadlines.
- Utilizing Productivity Peaks: Recognizing that my analytical capabilities peak in the early hours, I scheduled data analysis and detail-oriented tasks for the morning. This ensured that I tackled the most challenging aspects of the evaluation when my focus was sharpest.
- Implementing Focused Time Blocks: To maintain momentum and ensure thoroughness, I implemented focused time blocks. During these periods, I isolated myself from potential distractions, dedicating complete attention to the task at hand. This technique was pivotal in allowing me to delve deeper into the analysis, enhancing both the quality and speed of my work.[*]
- Strategic Breaks and Review Sessions: After intense work sessions, I scheduled short breaks to clear my mind and refocus. Additionally, I used end-of-day review sessions to assess the day's work, make necessary adjustments, and prepare for the next day. This helped not only in catching potential oversights early but also in maintaining a steady pace throughout the project duration.

By aligning task execution with my productivity cycles and rigorously managing my work schedule, the project was completed more efficiently than anticipated. Not only did this approach save time but it

---

[*] I To learn more about 'focused time blocks', see Newport, Cal. 2016. Deep Work: Rules for Focused Success in a Distracted World(Grand Central Publishing), page 226

also allowed for a thorough review and refinement phase, significantly enhancing the project's quality.

Integrating Freedom Within Structured Planning for Individual Productivity

Just as we've applied the Agile Equilibrium Framework at organizational and team levels, the principle of freedom is indeed equally crucial at the individual level. This involves allowing for flexibility within the structure of one's daily planning.

What does this look like in practice? It means that while it's essential to have a structured plan for productivity—perhaps organized meticulously on a tool like Trello—there should also be room to adapt based on personal needs and insights that arise throughout the day.

For example, if I have a specific scheduled day but find myself feeling unusually fatigued, I push myself to take a longer break to "refresh." This isn't just about resting; it's about optimizing performance for when I return to my tasks. Similarly, if I am working on a prioritized task but suddenly have a breakthrough idea on a different project, I find it beneficial to have the flexibility to pivot and capitalize on that insight, as long as it contributes to overall productivity.

The approach emphasizes that while structure is essential for maintaining both focus and organization, the freedom to adapt based on personal energy levels and emerging opportunities is equally important. This balance ensures that I am not only productive but also responsive to the dynamic nature of creative and intellectual work.

Adapting Agile Equilibrium Principles for Individual Productivity in Corporate Environments

I believe that in more traditional or less structured environments, where autonomy might be restricted and processes rigid, *employees can still find ways to implement personal productivity hacks.*

The following hacks could indeed be crucial for individuals seeking to maintain their effectiveness and job satisfaction despite the constraints of their work environment:

- Personal Time Management: Even in a rigid schedule, employees can use small windows of time effectively. Techniques such as the Pomodoro Technique, where work is broken into short, intense intervals followed by brief breaks, can be helpful. This method allows you to maintain concentration and energy levels throughout the day, even when the broader work environment is not conducive to such practices.
- Creating Personal Workflows: Employees can develop personal mini-systems or workflows that help streamline their tasks. This could involve organizing emails, setting specific times for checking communications, or using digital tools to manage tasks and deadlines, even if there aren't broader organizational tools available.
- Microplanning: In environments where long-term planning is challenging due to organizational flux, focusing on daily or weekly planning can provide a sense of control and direction. Employees can set clear, achievable goals for each day or week, allowing for adjustments as needed, based on the workplace dynamics.
- Leveraging Quiet Hours: Identifying and capitalizing on quiet hours at work (early mornings or late afternoons, for example) can allow for undisturbed, productive time. During these periods, employees can tackle the most challenging tasks or those requiring deep concentration.

While these individual strategies are essential, it is important to mention that organizations need to further empower their workforce by implementing structured flexibility, accommodating diverse working styles, and promoting efficiency by, for instance, considering the following dimensions

- Flexible Work Arrangements: Empowering employees with options such as remote work to decide how they best work. This flexibility helps individuals optimize their productivity by allowing them to work during their natural energy peaks.
- Distraction Management: Adopting policies such as visual signals for "do not disturb" moments to minimize interruptions. Simple, visual indicators can help maintain focus, especially in open office settings or where ad hoc requests are common.
- Enhanced Coaching and Onboarding: Providing guidance on time management and productivity strategies during onboarding and through continuous professional development. Effective coaching should also address the question of how to work autonomously within the organization's framework, encouraging employees to develop personal strategies that align with corporate goals.
- Promoting Individual Strategy Development: Encouraging employees to identify and use personal productivity hacks that suit their roles. Workshops or team-sharing sessions can be invaluable, providing a platform for exchanging ideas that enhance personal and team productivity.

Conclusion

Incorporating the Agile Equilibrium Framework into personal workflows is essential for balancing structured planning with the flexibility needed to foster creativity and productivity. By adopting tailored strategies such as utilizing planning tools, setting clear goals, and aligning tasks with productivity peaks, individuals can navigate the challenges of both traditional and freelance work environments effectively.

These principles are not only applicable at the organizational level but are also vital for individual success. Integrating freedom within structured planning and employing personal productivity hacks in rigid corporate environments can significantly enhance job satisfaction and efficiency. Ultimately, fostering an adaptable approach to time management and workflow can lead to sustained productivity and a more fulfilling work experience.

CHAPTER 7

Driving Change: Leadership and Learning

The Agile Equilibrium: Blending Agility With Structure in a Rapidly Changing World

We find ourselves at a pivotal moment, in an era where emerging technologies such as AI, blockchain, and the Internet of Things are not just advancing rapidly but are also fundamentally pushing us to change the ways we work. These technologies offer tremendous opportunities for innovation and efficiency, enabling us to tackle problems in ways that were previously unimaginable. They have the potential to enhance data processing capabilities, improve decision-making, and foster the creation of new business models, pushing organizations to adapt to more agile and innovative operational approaches.

Simultaneously, we face complex global challenges such as climate change, which require us to rethink traditional methods and push toward more collaborative practices. As these environmental issues demand innovative solutions, organizations must pivot from old methodologies to more adaptive approaches.

Many traditional organizations struggle with the agility needed to adapt to these fast-evolving technologies and to address today's complex challenges. They often lean too heavily on rigid structures, which can stifle innovation and slow down responsiveness. Conversely, *start-ups, while typically more nimble and flexible, often miss the opportunity to work effectively due to a lack of necessary structure, leading to inefficiencies and misaligned objectives.*

This dynamic landscape underscores the urgent need for a balanced approach. We need to reimagine the way in which we work as teams and as groups of teams (or organizations). The agile equilibrium offers a framework to think about how to integrate flexibility with structure, allowing teams and entire organizations to remain adaptable yet focused. This balance enables companies to respond swiftly to technological advances and market changes while maintaining a clear vision and strong governance.

By adopting an agile equilibrium, organizations and teams can harness the potential of emerging technologies to drive business success and adapt their work practices to address new challenges and societal demands effectively. This approach not only enhances operational efficiency but also fosters a culture of continuous improvement and innovation, which is crucial for thriving in today's complex, fast-paced business environment. In essence, achieving this balance allows organizations to combine.

Structure and Freedom in Great Companies

The balance between structure and freedom isn't just a theory—*it's a reality being practiced by many great companies across various sectors, not just in tech.* With their good practices, these companies exemplify what we call the agile equilibrium, a blend of discipline and autonomy that fosters innovation and adaptability. At the core of these organizations lies the understanding that discipline isn't about restriction but about establishing clear boundaries that provide direction. This structured guidance is essential as it ensures a definitive purpose while simultaneously allowing creativity and autonomy to flourish.

This balanced approach empowers these companies to innovate rapidly and respond adaptively to changes and challenges in their industries. It creates an environment where employees are encouraged to experiment and take initiative within a framework that aligns their efforts with the company's overall strategic objectives. By fostering such a culture, organizations not only boost their internal innovation capabilities but also enhance their competitive edge in the market.

Moreover, this agile equilibrium ensures that both leaders and team members have a clear understanding of their roles and contributions. Leaders set visions and expectations, while teams develop solutions that align with these goals. This clear alignment helps in minimizing misunderstandings and streamlining processes, ensuring that the organization remains agile and efficient despite the complexities of modern business landscapes.

Structure and Freedom in High-Performing Teams

The balance between structure and freedom is crucial not just for organizations but also for high-performing teams within them. Whether part of great companies, start-ups, or traditional organizations, the Agile Equilibrium Framework ensures that teams have enough autonomy to foster creativity and innovation while providing a clear framework that aligns their efforts with the organization's strategic goals.

Teams that effectively balance these elements can quickly adapt to new challenges and opportunities, enhancing their performance and contributing significantly to the organization's success. For instance, a start-up team developing a new product feature can benefit from the freedom to experiment and iterate on their ideas while adhering to structured timelines and objectives. This approach allows them to innovate more effectively and align their outcomes with broader business goals.

Even in traditional organizations, teams that operate with a degree of autonomy within clear organizational directives can contribute to modernizing and evolving these entities. This balance promotes a sense of ownership among team members and drives them to achieve exceptional results, proving that even within rigid structures, there can be pockets of innovation and efficiency.

By applying these principles, teams across all types of organizations can achieve a high level of performance, demonstrating that an interplay between structure and freedom is crucial for fostering environments where creativity, efficiency, and strategic alignment coexist. This balance is not merely beneficial; it is essential for teams striving to excel in an increasingly complex and fast-paced business world.

Placing People at the Center of Organizations

As we have seen in this book, there is a fundamental connection between the organizational framework, team dynamics, and individual contributions—all of which are interconnected and mutually reinforcing. Organizations must foster a culture and develop practices that not only benefit teams but also consider individual needs, ensuring that each person's way of working harmoniously integrates into the overall operational mechanism. *One of the most urgent messages here is the importance of placing people at the center of organizations.*

At the end of the day, it is the responsibility of organizations to cultivate an environment where individual empowerment is not just encouraged but systematically integrated into the organizational framework. Recognizing and supporting individual work styles and personal productivity within the collective context is crucial for achieving holistic success. A culture that adapts to and supports individual differences within a structured framework allows for enhanced personal satisfaction and productivity, which, in turn, boosts team effectiveness and drives organizational achievements.

By developing practices that align individual strengths with team goals and organizational objectives, companies can create a dynamic where the agile equilibrium extends to every level of operation.

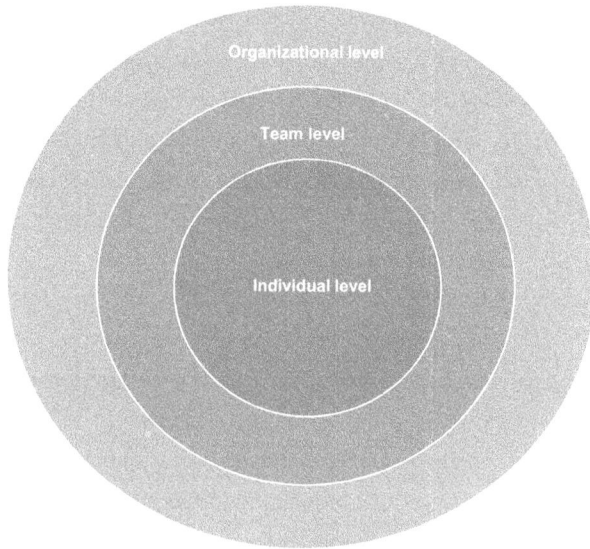

Figure 7.1 Connection between the different levels

Source: Developed by the author

This approach not only enhances the well-being and productivity of individuals but also ensures that the organization as a whole can adapt, innovate, and succeed in a competitive landscape.

Figure 7.1 visually represents the interconnected nature of individual, team, and organizational levels. It highlights how these three dimensions are mutually reinforcing and integral to achieving the agile equilibrium discussed throughout this book. The innermost circle represents individuals, whose empowerment and productivity form the foundation for effective teams, while teams, in turn, drive organizational success. This layered approach underscores the need for organizations to align practices that support individuals, foster collaboration within teams, and achieve broader organizational objectives.

Embracing Diversity in Approaches to Organizational and Team Performance

In our discussion, we've also underscored a crucial point: *The path for an organization to become more nimble and agile is not a one-size-fits-all formula but a continual process of trial, adaptation, and refinement.* Embracing a variety of approaches, experimenting with new methods, and continually adapting to emerging challenges and opportunities are essential steps on the path to sustained success and innovation. Each organization (and team within) must chart its own course, drawing on the broad principles of agile equilibrium while adjusting them to fit their particular context and objectives.

Also, change can originate from any level within an organization. This book has shown how performing teams can be successfully developed, even within the constraints of more traditional organizations. For example, it is possible to foster high-performing teams by implementing strategic "hacks" or targeted adjustments at the project level. These interventions did not necessitate a complete overhaul of the existing organizational framework. Instead, they introduced a balanced, context-specific approach that enhanced team dynamics and performance.

By selectively applying these agile principles, organizations can encourage a culture of innovation and flexibility. This strategic infusion of agility at the team level can act as a catalyst, setting the stage for broader organizational changes over time. It proves that transformative change does not always require top-down directives; instead, it can be incrementally achieved through thoughtful, localized changes, which accumulate to yield significant impacts.

Developing Progressive Leadership: Fostering Change and Inspiring Others

This dynamic of change within the organization and team resonates closely with *a progressive concept of leadership, which is less about holding a position of authority, and more about fostering change and inspiring others.* Effective leadership is about recognizing the potential for improvement across the organization and empowering individuals to drive the necessary change. This view of leadership is crucial, as it emphasizes the importance of initiative and responsibility, illustrating that anyone in the organization can lead change, irrespective of their formal job title.

This concept of leadership involves taking responsibility to achieve a purpose and motivate others, even in a context of uncertainty. For instance, in companies like those mentioned in our discussion, we see natural leaders taking initiatives without needing formal approval or authorization.

Leaders in these settings set the example, not through lavish expenditure or grand gestures, but through their integrity and commitment to the organization's values.

Building leadership capacity is critical, particularly in start-ups, as they transition from phases where the founders are the primary problem-solvers to stages where sustainable leadership must be cultivated. As Jeff Weiner (former CEO of LinkedIn) suggests, as companies scale up, it becomes imperative to hire or develop new leaders, to prevent a bottleneck at the top, where founders can become overwhelmed with decision-making.

If leaders are crucial for organizations and teams to change and improve, then how do we create this kind of leaders?

Developing adaptive and empowering leadership involves a multifaceted approach that encompasses education, hiring practices, and a broader cultural shift within organizations and society. Here's how we can build this kind of leadership, based on literature and best practices:

- Education and Training: It's essential to provide ongoing education and training in management and leadership. This includes not only formal educational programs but also continuous on-the-job training and development opportunities that focus on real-world applications. Leadership development programs should emphasize critical thinking, ethical decision-making, and the ability to adapt to changing circumstances.
- Hiring Practices: When hiring, it's crucial to look for candidates who are not only intelligent but also quick learners. Intelligence should be broadly defined to include emotional intelligence, which enables leaders to understand and manage their own emotions and those of others. Look for traits such as self-motiva-

tion and self-discipline, as these are indicative of individuals who can thrive in self-organizing environments.

- A Cultural Shift in Organizations: Foster a culture that values autonomy and trusts the capabilities of all team members. This involves moving away from traditional command-and-control models to ones that encourage initiative and are tolerant of failure. By allowing employees to take calculated risks and possibly fail, organizations can cultivate a learning environment where leaders can emerge naturally.

- Rethinking the Educational System: The development of leadership qualities should start much earlier in life. It's a societal issue that involves rethinking how the educational system prepares individuals for the workplace. Educators and parents should encourage independence, critical thinking, and problem-solving from a young age. This shift will help cultivate a generation that is comfortable with autonomy and empowered to lead.

- Leadership as a Role, Not a Rank: Reinforce the idea that leadership does not necessarily come with a title or a specific position within the hierarchy. Leadership is about taking responsibility, and motivating others in a context of uncertainty. By demonstrating that everyone can exhibit leadership qualities in different settings, organizations can inspire all employees to embrace leadership roles.

- Coaching and Mentorship: For start-ups and growing businesses, it's particularly important to transition from founder-led problem-solving to a leadership style that scales. This can be achieved through mentoring and coaching, where experienced leaders guide less experienced ones, helping them to develop the skills needed to lead effectively.

- Building Systems for Self-Organization: Encourage the development of systems that support self-organization. This might include decentralized decision-making frameworks or platforms that allow employees to initiate projects and drive innovation without the need for extensive approvals.

A Call to Action: Transforming Organizations and Teams

The overarching message of this book is *a fervent call to action: we need to develop organizations and teams that are equipped to navigate the complexities of the 21st century.* The hierarchical management models of the past no longer suit the pace and intricacies of today's global economy. We are at a crucial juncture where there is an urgent need for a movement toward organizational structures that prioritize autonomy, flexibility, and human-centric leadership.

What I advocate is a profound transformation in the way organizations and teams operate. The path to organizational greatness lies in mastering the delicate balance between structure and freedom, creating environments where creativity, leadership, and innovation are not merely encouraged but are integral to the organizational fabric. As we look toward the future, it is clear that adapting our organizations to meet contemporary demands is not merely beneficial—it is essential.

My hope is that this book will serve as a catalyst for positive change, guiding both individuals and organizations toward greater agility, empowerment, and satisfaction. This aspiration aligns with my vision of transforming organizational cultures to better support the human elements within them. Ultimately, the book is designed to make a meaningful difference in the way organizations operate, and individuals within them flourish, steering us toward a future where our workplaces are not only productive but also nurturing and inspiring.

Notes

My Story

1. Alcacer, Khanna and Snively. "The Rise and Fall of Nokia".
2. Hoffman, Kohut and Prusak. *Smart Mission NASA's Lessons for Managing Knowledge, People, and Projects.*
3. Azhar. *The Exponential Age.*
4. Ries. *The Lean Startup: How Today's Entrepreneurs Use Continuous Innovation to Create Radically Successful Businesses.*
5. Laloux. *Reinventing Organizations: A Guide to Creating Organizations Inspired by the Next Stage of Human Consciousness.* p.13.
6. Conley. *Peak: How Great Companies Get Their Mojo from Maslow.*
7. Conley. *Peak.* p. 229.
8. Gallup. *State of the Global Workplace: 2023 Report.*

Chapter 1

1. Jim. *Good to Great: Why Some Companies Make the Leap...And Others Don't.*
2. Hastings and Meyer. *No Rules Rules: Netflix and the Culture of Reinvention,* p. 122.

Chapter 2

1. Laloux, F. *Reinventing Organizations,* pp.1–9.
2. Godin, S. *Tribes: We Need You to Lead Us,* pp.12–14.
3. McKinsey & Company. *Leading Agile Transformation: The New Capabilities Leaders Need to Build 21st-century Organizations,* p.5.
4. Laloux, F. *Reinventing Organizations,* pp.173–193.
5. Pink, D. *Drive: The Surprising Truth About What Motivates Us.*

Chapter 4

1. Getz, I., and Carney, B. M. *Freedom, Inc..*
2. Getz, I., and Carney, B. M. *Freedom, Inc.,* p.61.

3. Nadella, S. *Hit Refresh: The Quest to Rediscover Microsoft's Soul and Imagine a Better Future for Everyone*, p.100.

4. Sinek, S. *Start with Why: How Great Leaders Inspire Everyone to Take Action.*

5. Conley, C. *Peak.*

6. McCann, C. "Scaling LinkedIn: Jeff Weiner - Class 19 Notes Stanford CS183C."

7. Sheridan, R. *Joy, Inc.: How We Built a Workplace People Love*, pp.87–107.

8. Semler, R. "Managing Without Managers." *Harvard Business Review* (September–October 1989).

9. Hempel, J. "This Company Lets Employees Take Charge: Buurtzorg." *Harvard Business School Working Knowledge.*

10. Zobrist, J.-F. *L'entreprise Libérée Par Le Petit Patron Naïf Et Paresseux.*

11. Bernstein, E., and Bunch, J. "The Zappos Holacracy Experiment." *Harvard Business Review.*

12. Semler, R. "Managing Without Managers."

13. Cruth, M. "Discover the Spotify Model." Available at: https://www.atlassian.com/agile/agile-at-scale/spotify.

14. Apolitical. "No Managers, No Bureaucracy: How the Netherlands Improved Care for Less." Available at: https://apolitical.co.

15. Gore, W. L. "Gore Recognized as One of the World's Best Multinational Workplaces by Great Place to Work."

16. Forbes. "W. L. Gore & Associates."

17. Sutton, R. I., and Rao, H. *The Friction Project: How Smart Leaders Make the Right Things Easier and the Wrong Things Harder.*

18. Sheridan, R. *Joy, Inc..*

19. Sheridan, R. *Joy, Inc.*, pp.153–165.

20. Hoffman, E., Kohut, M., and Prusak, L. *Smart Mission: NASA's Lessons for Managing Knowledge, People, and Projects.*

21. Doerr, J. *Measure What Matters: How Google, Bono, and the Gates Foundation Rock the World with OKRs.*

22. Sheridan, R. *Joy, Inc..*

23. McCann, C. "Scaling LinkedIn: Jeff Weiner - Class 19 Notes Stanford CS183C."

24. Hamel, G., and Zanini, M. *Humanocracy: Creating Organizations as Amazing as the People Inside Them.*

25. Sheridan, R. *Joy, Inc..*

26. Ek, D. "Organizational Changes." Available at: https://www.spotify.com.

27. Getz, I., and Carney, B. M. *Freedom, Inc.*, p.149.

28. Jay, A. *Corporation Man.*

29. Rigby, D. K., Sutherland, J., and Noble, A. "Agile at Scale." *Harvard Business Review*. Available at: https://hbr.org/2018/04/agile-at-scale.

Chapter 5

1. Isaacson, W. *Elon Musk.*

2. Bezos, J. "2016 Letter to Shareholders." Available at: https://www.aboutamazon.com.

3. Dalio, R. *Principles: Life and Work*, p.372.

4. Knapp, J., Zeratsky, J., and Kowitz, B. *Sprint: How to Solve Big Problems and Test New Ideas in Just Five Days.*

5. Sheridan, R. *Joy, Inc..*

6. Forbes Communications Council. "Why and How Every Company Should Use Amazon's Six-Page Memo Format." *Forbes*. Available at: https://www.forbes.com.

7. Duhigg, C. "What Google Learned from Its Quest to Build the Perfect Team." *The New York Times*. Available at: https://www.nytimes.com.

8. Sinek, S. "Performance vs. Trust." Available at: https://www.youtube.com.

9. Edmondson, A. *The Fearless Organization: Creating Psychological Safety in the Workplace for Learning, Innovation, and Growth.*

10. Catmull, E. "Inside the Pixar Braintrust." *FastCompany*. Available at: https://www.fastcompany.com.

References

Andrews, Matt, Lant Pritchett, and Michael Woolcock. 2018. "PDIA Toolkit: A DIY Approach to Solving Complex Problems." *Harvard Kennedy School, Center for International Development.*

Apolitical. 2024. "No Managers, No Bureaucracy: How the Netherlands Improved Care for Less."

Atlassian. 2023. "OKRs: Set, Achieve, and Track Them with Trello." www.atlassian.com/blog/trello/okrs-set-achieve-track-trello.

Azhar, A. 2022. *The Exponential Age.* New York: Penguin.

Bezos, J. 2016. "2016 Letter to Shareholders, Amazon.com, Inc." www.aboutamazon.com/news/company-news/2016-letter-to-shareholders.

Catmull, Ed. 2014. "Inside the Pixar Braintrust." *Fastcompany.*

Collins, J. 2001. *Good to Great: Why Some Companies Make the Leap … and Others Don't.* NY, New York: HarperBusiness.

Conley, C. 2007. *Peak: How Great Companies Get Their Mojo From Maslow.* San Francisco: Jossey-Bass.

Cruth, M. 2024. "Discover the Spotify Model." www.atlassian.com/agile/agile-at-scale/spotify.

Dalio, R. 2017. *Principles: Life and Work.* NY, New York: Simon & Schuster.

Doerr, J. 2018. *Measure What Matters.* New York: Portfolio.

Duhigg, C. 2016. "What Google Learned From Its Quest to Build the Perfect Team." *The New York Times.* www.nytimes.com/2016/02/28/magazine/what-google-learned-from-its-quest-to-build-the-perfect-team.html.

Edmonson, A. 2018. *The Fearless Organization: Creating Psychological Safety in the Workplace for Learning, Innovation, and Growth.* Wiley.

Forbes Communications Council. 2022. "Why and How Every Company Should Use Amazon's Six-Page Memo Format." *Forbes.* www.forbes.com/sites/forbescommunicationscouncil/2022/08/30/why-and-how-every-company-should-use-amazons-six-page-memo-format/.

Gallup. 2023. *State of the Global Workplace.* 2023 Report.

Geetz, I. and B.M. Carney. 2009. *Freedom, Inc.* NY, New York: Crown Business.

Godin, S. 2008. *Tribes: We Need You to Lead Us.* NY, New York: Portfolio.

Hamel, G., and M. Zaninin. 2020. *Humanocracy: Creating Organizations as Amazing as the People Inside Them.* Harvard Business Review Press.

Hastings, R., and M. Erin. 2020. *No Rules Rules: Netflix and the Culture of Reinvention.* NY, New York: Penguin Press.

Hempel, J. 2023. "This Company Lets Employees Take Charge: Buurtzorg." *Harvard Business School Working Knowledge.*

Isaacson, W. 2023. *Elon Musk.* NY, New York: Simon & Schuster.

Jay, A. 1973. *Corporation Man.* Pocket Books.

Knapp, J., John Z., and B., Kowitz. 2016. *Sprint: How to Solve Big Problems and Test New Ideas in Just Five Days.* NY, New York: Simon & Schuster.

Laloux, F. 2014. *Reinventing Organizations: A Guide to Creating Organizations Inspired by the Next Stage of Human Consciousness.* Brussels: Nelson Parker.

McCann, C. 2015. "Scaling LinkedIn: Jeff Weiner—Class 19 Notes Stanford CS183C." *LinkedIn.*

McKinsey & Company. 2018. *Leading Agile Transformation: The New Capabilities Leaders Need to Build 21st-Century Organizations.* NY, New York: McKinsey & Company.

Meyer, Erin. 2014. *The Culture Map: Breaking Through the Invisible Boundaries of Global Business.* New York: PublicAffairs.

Ministère de la santé publique, République du Niger. 2017. Guide national pour l'application de l'approche par les résultats rapides (RRI)

Nadella, S. 2017. *Hit Refresh: The Quest to Rediscover Microsoft's Soul and Imagine a Better Future for Everyone.* NY, New York: Harper Business.

Newport, C. 2016. *Deep Work: Rules for Focused Success in a Distracted World.* New York: Grand Central Publishing.

Pink, D. 2009. *Drive: The Surprising Truth About What Motivates Us.* NY, New York: Riverhead Books.

Ries, E. 2011. *The Lean Startup: How Today's Entrepreneurs Use Continuous Innovation to Create Radically Successful Businesses.* NY, New York: Crown Business.

Schmidt, E., and J. Rosenberg. 2014. *How Google Works.* NY, New York: Grand Central Publishing.

Semler, R. 1989. "Managing Without Managers." *Harvard Business Review.*

Sheridan, R. 2015. *Joy, Inc.: How We Built a Workplace People Love.* NY, New York: Portfolio Penguin.

Sinek, S. 2009. *Start With Why: How Great Leaders Inspire Everyone to Take Action.* NY, New York: Portfolio.

Sutton, R.I., and R. Huggy. 2024. *The Friction Project: How Smart Leaders Make the Right Things Easier and the Wrong Things Harder.* St. Martin's Press.

Zobrist, J.-F. 2015. *L'entreprise libérée par le petit patron naïf et paresseux.* France: François Bourin Éditeur.

About the Author

Tommaso Balbo di Vinadio is an instructor, entrepreneur, and development specialist with over 20 years of experience at the intersection of academia, public service, and the private sector—including start-ups. Beginning his career in evaluating and developing large-scale public sector programs, Tommaso has progressively shifted his focus toward organizational innovation and the creation of high-performing teams. He currently resides in France, where he also teaches at SciencesPo, bringing his blend of practical and academic insights to the next generation of leaders.

Index

OTHER TITLES IN THE HUMAN RESOURCE MANAGEMENT AND ORGANIZATIONAL BEHAVIOR COLLECTION

Michael J. Provitera and Michael Edmondson, Editors

- *Successful Self-Leadership* by Tim Baker
- *Nice Guys Finish Last And Other Workplace Lies,* by John Ruffa
- *Understanding and Using AI* by Daniel O. Livvarcin and Yacouba Traoré
- *The Leadership Edge* by Michael B. Ross and Mike Shaw
- *Business and Management in the Age of Intangible Capitalism* by Hamid Yeganeh
- *Ignite All* by The Fusion Team
- *(Re)Value* by Adam Wallace and Adam Wallace
- *Dysfunctional Organizations* by David D. Van Fleet
- *The Negotiation Edge* by Michael Saksa
- *Applied Leadership* by Sam Altawil
- *Forging Dynasty Businesses* by Chuck Violand
- *How the Harvard Business School Changed the Way We View Organizations* by Jay W. Lorsch
- *Managing Millennials* by Jacqueline Cripps
- *Personal Effectiveness* by Lucia Strazzeri
- *Catalyzing Transformation* by Sandra Waddock

Concise and Applied Business Books

The Collection listed above is one of 30 business subject collections that Business Expert Press has grown to make BEP a premiere publisher of print and digital books. Our concise and applied books are for...

- Professionals and Practitioners
- Faculty who adopt our books for courses
- Librarians who know that BEP's Digital Libraries are a unique way to offer students ebooks to download, not restricted with any digital rights management
- Executive Training Course Leaders
- Business Seminar Organizers

Business Expert Press books are for anyone who needs to dig deeper on business ideas, goals, and solutions to everyday problems. Whether one print book, one ebook, or buying a digital library of 110 ebooks, we remain the affordable and smart way to be business smart. For more information, please visit www.businessexpertpress.com, or contact sales@businessexpertpress.com.

www.ingramcontent.com/pod-product-compliance
Lightning Source LLC
Chambersburg PA
CBHW061325220326
41599CB00026B/5041